# Flowers of Heaven

# FLOWERS OF HEAVEN
DEBBIE MORRISON

A FAMILY'S STORY OF
# LOVE AND LOSS
ON COLPOY'S BAY

COPYRIGHT © 2024 DEBORAH MORRISON

All rights reserved. No part of this book may be reproduced, distributed or transmitted in any form without prior written permission from the author, except for brief passages for the purpose of a review.

www.debbiemorrison.net

Images: Non-personal photos printed with permission. Rights reserved.

*Flowers of Heaven: A Family's Story of Love and Loss on Colpoy's Bay*
Debbie Morrison

Published in 2024
Printed in the United States of America

1. Colpoy's Bay (Ont.) history 2. Women's history 20th century Canada 3. Georgian Bay region 4. Wiarton history 5. Kastner family 6. Ontario history 20th century 7. Mental health history—Canada 20th century.

Book and cover design by Debbie Morrison

Cover image: Government Dock at Colpoy's Bay, photo by Telfer, 1923; inset image Isobel and Gretchen Kastner, see page 14

Inside image [previous page]: Colpoy's Bay, photo by Don McCallum, 2016

*For my family and Victor.*

"When I was young I believed that 'nonfiction' meant 'true.' But you read a history written in, say, 1920 and a history of the same events written in 1995 and they're very different. There may not be one Truth— there may be several truths—but saying that is not to say that reality doesn't exist."

— MARGARET ATWOOD, 1997

## AUTHOR'S NOTE

THIS IS A STORY about a real person, my grandmother, Gretchen Kastner-Doull, who drowned in Colpoy's Bay on the night of May 27, 1941. She left behind two children—a six-year-old boy and a fourteen-month-old girl; a mother, a father, four siblings; and a husband who was seeking a divorce. What follows is more than the tragic story of a woman who committed suicide; it's about a notable family from Wiarton and a vibrant, confident woman who went for a walk and never returned.

*Flowers of Heaven* is set on one day, May 28, 1941, the day Gretchen's body was found, and is told through the voices of those impacted by Gretchen's death: her family, her doctor in Wiarton, the police chief who discovered her body, and Mabel, Wiarton's newspaper editor. The characters come to life in the story with fictionalized narrative and internal dialogues—a writing style known as "stream of consciousness." This technique, introduced by author Virginia Woolf, gives readers a glimpse into the lives and inner thoughts of a story's characters. I chose this style to make the story more engaging and for another reason, which has to do with Woolf herself. The latter is revealed within the story.

The characters in *Flowers of Heaven* were all real people, apart from Doctor Burns, who is portrayed as Gretchen's doctor in Montreal. It is certain that Gretchen had a doctor while she lived in Montreal, but his or her identity is lost to history. The events in the book all occurred within Gretchen's lifetime and are based on research gathered from family documents, interviews, photographs, journal articles, archives from the Bruce County Museum, the website Postcards From the Bay, and *The Family Histories*, a document authored by Robert (Bob) Kastner, Gretchen's nephew. I did, however, take creative liberties with the dialogue in order to create an engaging story.

During my research, I also learned about events that happened within Canada during Gretchen's era, specifically in Ontario and Quebec. These, I felt, should be included. Family stories, especially tragedies, are influenced by the social, political, and cultural narratives of the day. The "Afterword" fleshes these out and includes startling facts about Canadian divorce laws, treatments for mental illness, attitudes towards alcohol, and others. It touches on women's rights in Canada from the 1920s through the 1940s—specifically, women's agency in marriage, politics, and work, and how the medical community treated women differently from men. It concludes with a brief history of Wiarton, where Gretchen was born, grew up, and was married, giving further insight into Gretchen's story. *Flowers of Heaven* highlights progress in women's rights and medicine but also underscores the challenges we still face.

My aim with *Flowers of Heaven: A Family's Story of Love and Loss on Colpoy's Bay* is to provide a glimpse into how people, families, and women experienced life in Gretchen's era—how it felt to experience loss, love, emotional pain, and joy. I share this story with the best of intentions. Any and all errors are mine.

# TABLE OF CONTENTS

Prologue .................................................................................15
Map of Colpoy's Bay ..............................................................19
Gretchen's Family 1941........................................................ 20

## CHAPTERS

*One*: Paul ............................................................................. 24
*Two*: Jack ............................................................................. 28
*Three*: Chief Boyle .............................................................. 36
*Four*: Dickie's Shadow ........................................................ 40
*Five*: Hillcrest ..................................................................... 47
*Six*: Doctor Stott ................................................................. 50
*Seven*: Gideon .................................................................... 55
*Eight*: Mabel ....................................................................... 60
*Nine*: Margaret ................................................................... 65
*Ten*: Gretchen ..................................................................... 73

Epilogue ............................................................................... 76
Afterword ............................................................................. 89

Acknowledgments ............................................................. 108
Image Details and Credits ................................................. 110
Bibliography ...................................................................... 112

Gretchen [right] and sister her Isobel. c 1929 – 1932

# PROLOGUE

I NEVER KNEW MY grandmother Gretchen. I thought Nini was my "real" grandmother. Nini, a twist on her name Nina that I gave her when I was two, was my mum's stepmother who was married to my grandfather, Pupi (who I also named at the age two). It wasn't until I heard an off-hand comment from Nini about Gretchen when I was eleven-years old that I found out otherwise. I don't remember the circumstances, but it didn't seem a big deal at the time, to Nini at least, that Gretchen had died when Mum was one and Mum's brother Hugh was six. Nini had married Pupi a year after Gretchen's death. I remember at the time trying to make sense of it. I wondered why Mum or my grandparents had never told me or my sisters about Gretchen.

In the years that followed I didn't learn much about Gretchen except for fragments of stories from Nini and Mum. One story Nini shared was how Gretchen left Mum and Hugh alone one night while she went for walk. How this could be? I wondered. How could a grown woman, a mother, leave her baby and small boy all alone? At that time, I was beginning to babysit. I couldn't imagine leaving an infant to fend for itself or a six-year-old for that matter.

Learning that Nini was my step-grandmother and hearing stories that my birth grandmother might have been unstable didn't disturb me as much as it might your average eleven-year-old. My world was already full of disturbing events. My parents divorced when I was six and my twin sisters four. My father remarried when I was eight. When I was ten, my sisters and I moved with

Mum and her new boyfriend to Nassau, Bahamas. We stayed for a year, then returned to Canada. They married shortly after we settled in Brampton, Ontario. Two years later, they divorced. This all happened by the time I was thirteen.

My grandfather never mentioned Gretchen or her family, the Kastners. Pupi was a closed shop, a loving grandparent (as was Nini), but not big on details. But the story I pieced together from Nini and Mum went something like this: Gretchen and my grandfather met at McGill University in Montreal and married shortly afterwards. Gretchen committed suicide when Mum was a baby and Hugh was six or seven years old. According to Mum, Hugh found Gretchen in the bathtub. Gretchen, according to Nini, was of unsound mind and would frequently leave the children with neighbours and disappear. My grandfather, according to both Nini and Mum, had asked Gretchen for a divorce so that he could marry Nini. They were having an affair. But the divorce never happened. Gretchen took her own life before it was ever finalized.

As I delved into the family history, I discovered that the stories were not all true. For one, Gretchen did not die in a bathtub. Second, Gretchen was not of an unsound mind but suffered from depression. These snippets reveal the problem with relying on oral stories to recreate the past. They are prone to embellishment. Narrators, like my mum, often add dramatic details for effect that leave a story falling somewhere along a continuum of truth and fiction. The stories about Gretchen went something like that. Part truth, part embellishment, part false. This led me to writing this book.

I wanted to find out the truth about Gretchen—what she was like, about her family (and mine), and what might have led to her death. I pored over documents, including birth and death certificates, my great-grandfather's will, newspaper articles, photographs, and written accounts by and about the Kastner family. I researched divorce laws in Canada, mental health disorders, treatments for depression, and logging—the industry that made my great-grandfather's career. One of the last living family members who remembered Gretchen was Paul Kastner; I interviewed him in 2016. I also visited the Kastner family home, Hillcrest, in Wiarton and researched the history of Wiarton and Colpoy's Bay.

Along the way, I encountered shocking facts—the restrictive nature of divorce laws in Canada, the lack of agency women experienced in Gretchen's era, and what life was like for women living in a small Ontario town. I wove these facts and others into the story to give it context and shape.

*Flowers of Heaven* took me several years to write. I originally intended to focus on Gretchen, but as my research expanded, I realized her story was inseparable from her family, the cities she lived in, and the values, politics, and religion of her era. For these reasons, I rewrote the book several times with the goal of creating more depth and meaning. I also recognized that it was the lives of the people around Gretchen who could tell the story best and who could give insight into what life was like for families and women living in Canada in the decades between 1920 and 1940.

In chapters two through nine, you will hear the voices of these characters and see the story through their eyes. In the "Epilogue," you will discover more about the characters, their lives after Gretchen died, and several curious events that occurred after her death. The last chapter, "Afterword," ties the story together, grounds it, and exposes relevant issues that are still with us today.

The names of characters in the story have not been changed; they are the same as they were used during each character's lifetime. The one exception is Gretchen's sister-in-law, who goes by the name "Cora" in the book. Her real name is Anne Cora Kastner (née Gardiner). She went by "Anne" in her lifetime, but I used her middle name to avoid confusion with Annie Kastner, Gretchen's mother.

With that said, I share with you *Flowers of Heaven: A Family's Story of Love and Loss on Colpoy's Bay.*

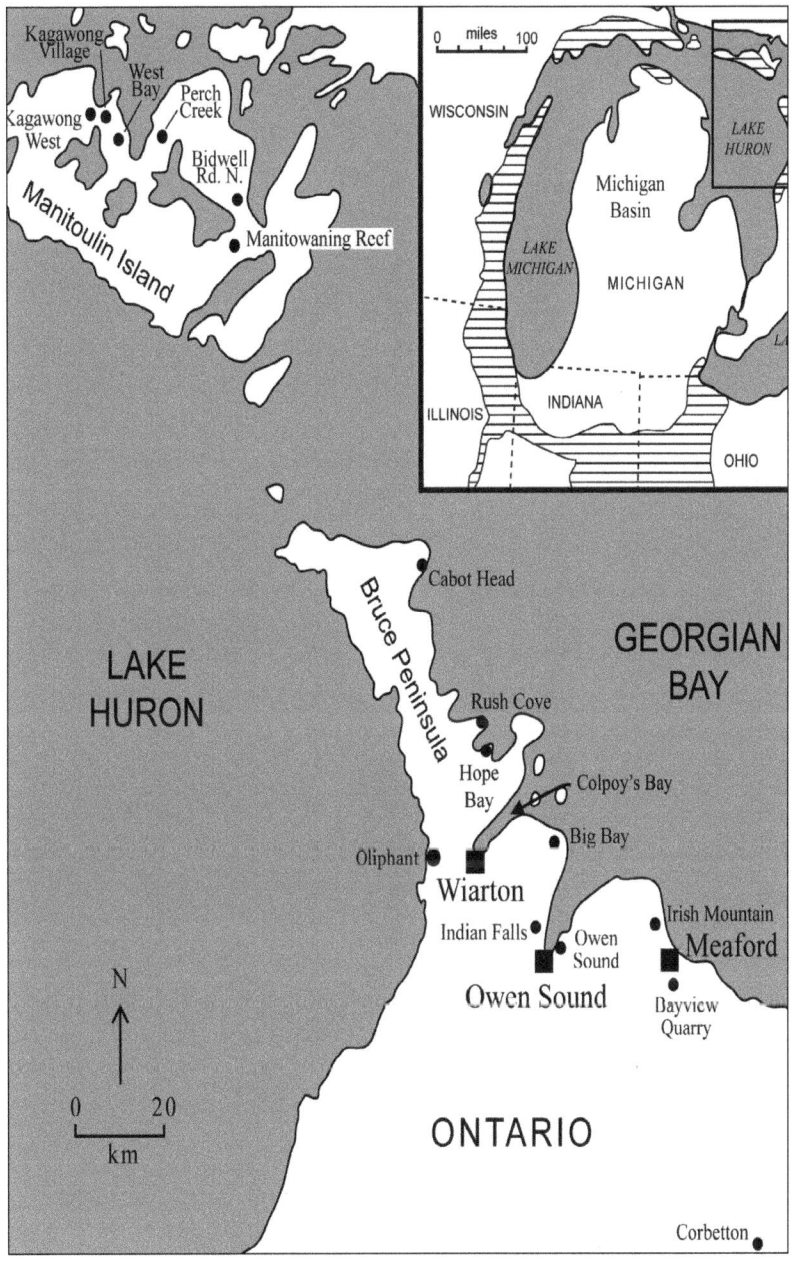

Map of Colpoy's Bay in relation to Wiarton and Georgian Bay [above]
Outline of The Great Lakes [left]

20 FLOWERS OF HEAVEN

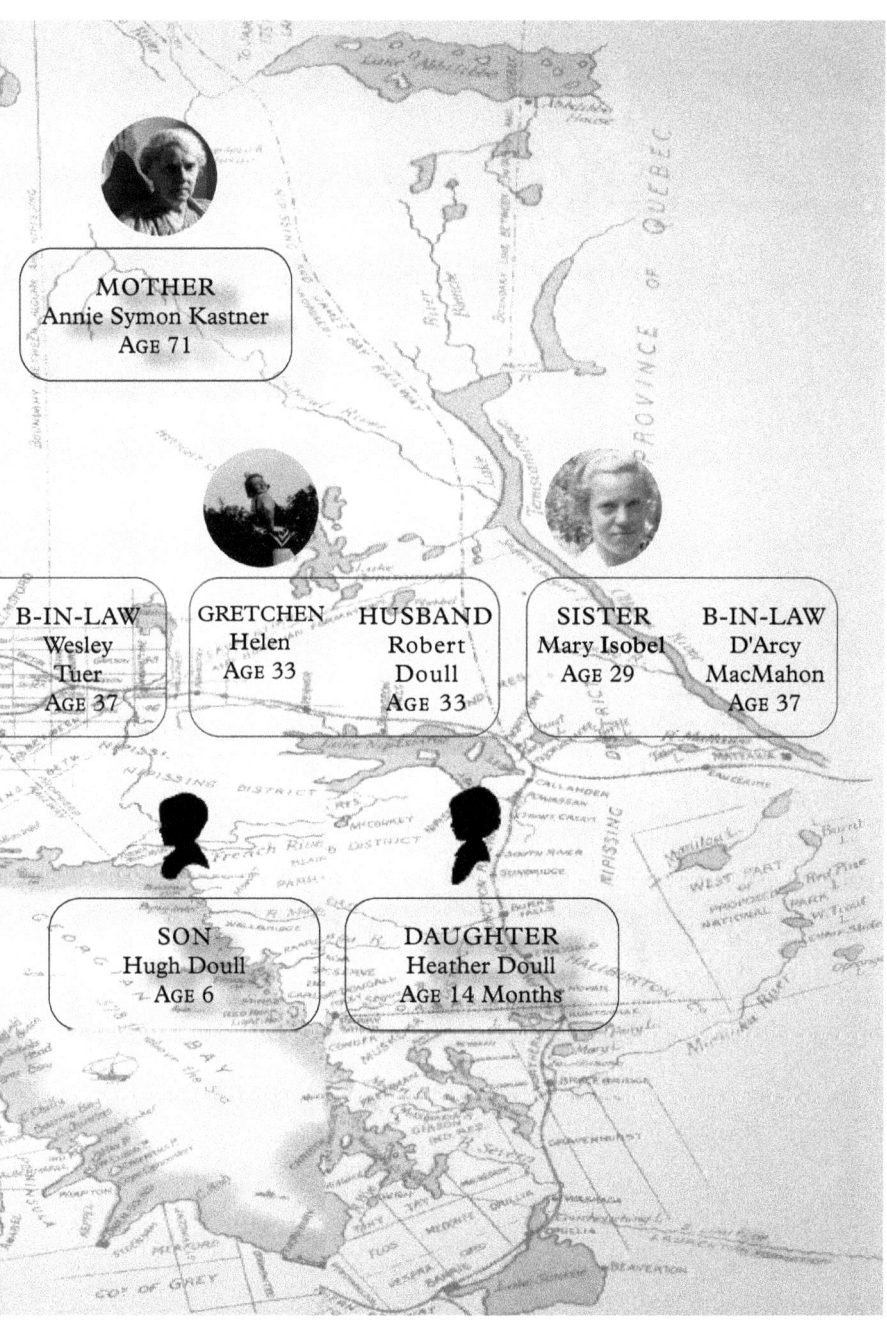

Kastner family on the front lawn of the family home, Hillcrest, 394 Gould Street, Wiarton. From left to right: Jack, Isobel, Margaret, Annie, Gretchen, Bernice, Gideon. c. 1926

CHAPTER ONE

# PAUL

"Paul... No school today—son, wake up—you're staying home today." Paul rolls over and opens his eyes. He was elated at the thought of no school—until he sees his dad's face. It looks tired, grey, and his eyes have red rims around them like he had been crying.

"Take care of your brother son."

His dad leans over and kisses his forehead. His lips are cool. Paul suddenly feels cold. He shivers and pulls up the bedsheets. He can hear his dad's footsteps on the stairs after he leaves his room, and the bang of the back door. Then, the low rumbling of the car and the familiar crunching sound of gravel from the tires.

It must be Aunt Gretchen he thought. She seemed sad last night. He had never seen anyone like it. She acted as if she were frozen. Her body was stiff, and she barely talked even when Dad had tried everything to cheer her up. But come to think of it, she did smile that one time —when Dad sang his favourite song from his lumber camp days.

Paul starts humming the tune his dad had sung the night before, then whispers the words under his breath.

"Come all you sons of freedom, and listen to my theme
Come all you roving lumberjacks that run the Saginaw streams

We'll cross the Tittabawassee where the mighty waters flow,
And we'll roam the wild woods over and once more a-lumbering go.
You may talk about your farms, your houses and fine places,
But pity not the shanty boys while dashing on their sleigh,
For around the good campfire at night we'll sing while wild winds blow,
And we'll roam the wild woods over and once more a-lumbering go."

Dad sings those songs a lot. He likes to tell me the story about how he wrote lumberjack on my birth certificate as his occupation. Dad said he had worked in lumber camps, cutting trees for Granddad's mill when I was born. It was hard work according to Dad. The axe from his lumberjack days is still in the basement, next to his gardening tools. He calls it the Black Prince. Dad says it was made in Montreal by a man who learned to make axes in England. It is his favourite tool, or so it seems the way that Dad talks about it. Every year when we chop down our Christmas tree, he brings it along and tells me the same story: *It's all about the first cut Paul. You must respect the tree—take as few cuts as possible. A lumberjack approaches every tree differently—each is unique as you or I.*

I think that Dad liked that job the best—the lumberjack job. He had lived in the woods away from Grandmother and Granddad for a long time. But it didn't sound like much fun. I wouldn't want to live so far away from home. But I think it made him happy. Not selling suits like he does now. Or when he worked at the furniture factory with Granddad.

Paul gets out of bed and pulls the curtains back. The sky is grey. It looks gloomy, but he notices that the colour green is everywhere. The trees are thick with leaves. Likely, he thinks, it's because it had been raining for days until yesterday. Paul goes back to his bed, lies down, and looks up at the ceiling.

I like it here now. This is the best place by far. The worst was after Dad left the furniture factory and we had to move to Cornwall. I hated it there. It was cold. I remember that time Bob's tongue got stuck on the frozen metal fence in the backyard. I was so mad; I had to miss my lacrosse game. I remember feeling sad a lot. But I don't think I was as sad as Aunt Gretchen is now. Last night was the saddest I have seen her since she came back to Wiarton. I think that's why Dad thought the car ride would be good for her, since it had been raining the day before. I'm glad Dad asked me to go with the grownups, and Bob had to stay with Heather and Hugh. I like Hugh and Heather much more than Bob—Heather especially. I like how she follows me around everywhere now that she is walking. I don't think Heather and Hugh have seen Uncle Robert since they moved back to Wiarton. I wonder if they miss him. I would miss my dad if it were me. Mum told me it is a divorce—a divorce from Uncle Robert that makes Aunt Gretchen so glum. She is going to be moving into the house across from Grandmother and Granddad's. Mum says she will be happier there. I wonder what happened. I remember hearing Dad and Mum talking and saying how Aunt Margaret was visiting too much when Aunt Gretchen and Uncle Robert lived in Montreal.

Paul gets up from bed and walks over to his dresser to get his clothes. He's glad he doesn't have to go to school, but knows his Mum will make him do schoolwork. He wonders when his dad will come back home.

Maybe Aunt Gretchen had gone to see Uncle Robert. He decides to tell his dad his theory when he comes home. Paul hopes that is where Aunt Gretchen went.

Paul [left] and Bob playing on the lawn of Hillcrest. Paul is holding a small child with curly blond hair, who is likely Heather, Gretchen's daughter. 1941, shortly before Gretchen's death.

CHAPTER TWO

# JACK

JACK IS AT THE long dock. Parked, his car faces Colpoy's Bay. He stares over the water. He loves how the bay changes drastically from still to tumultuous from one hour to the next, its deep blue colour—it reminds him of a blue sky on one of his good days. This morning, the water is bluish-grey, unsettled, and distraught.

"Damn, damn. Gretchen where are you?" Jack shouts out loud while hitting the steering wheel with the palms of his hands until they're numb. He stops, puts his hands under his armpits, crossing his arms tightly across his body.

He knew something was wrong last night. He had sensed it when he dropped Gretchen and his mother off at Hillcrest. He should have gone back; should have brought Gretchen back to his house. But Mother had been insistent—*All will be fine Jack; don't worry.* But she is not fine. Anyone can see that. Gretchen barely speaks. She acts as if she wants to be invisible. Maybe the drive through town and out to Oliphant by the cottage had made it worse. He had thought it would help. He had hoped Gretchen would cheer up when remembering the good times they had when they were kids—when they swam, played games, and spent long days outdoors. She was always happy, full of life.

Jack recalled how they had arranged themselves in the car yesterday afternoon: Gretchen with him in the front, Mother, Cora, and Paul in the back. They had rolled down the car windows, and Mother had waved enthusiastically to Margaret and the children when they left. For some reason, it had irritated him. Maybe he was thinking of Gretchen; he was sensitive to how people behaved around her. He wanted Gretch to get back to her old cheerful self; he didn't want anything to annoy her.

Jack visualized the route they took—down Mary Street, left onto Berford—past the shops, his store, and the movie theatre. Mother had talked incessantly, *Look Paul, Gone with the Wind is playing this weekend. Finally, it comes to Wiarton. Margaret and I saw it when we were in Toronto visiting your Aunt Isobel. Would you like to see it? Maybe Aunt Margaret can take you.* They had driven past the hotels and turned onto Division Street, then left on Bayview. He had wanted to give Gretchen a view of the Bay, since it had been such a beautiful day. He had parked along the roadside by one of the small docks. The Bay was stupendous; it glistened as the sun turned to burnt orange. But Gretchen had stared ahead with barely an acknowledgment. It was then that Jack decided to go to Oliphant and drive by the family cottage. Mother had protested at first but stopped when she glanced over at Gretchen's immobile profile. Jack remembered how Gretchen loved the summers at the cottage, especially the lake. He remembered the year when Gretchen and Bernice had entered the girls' water-running and sculling events at Oliphant's Camper's Association regatta. Bernice had won both—Gretchen had come in second. They had laughed afterwards. Both girls were competitive, but not with each other. Good swimmers they were, and athletes, as far as women go.

Jack recalled that it was through sports that Gretchen and Robert had met at McGill. Gretchen had been on the Women's Athletic Association at MacDonald's College and Robert on McGill's Soccer team. He remembered Robert telling him shortly after they had married: *Your sister enjoys the outdoors. I love that about her.* They had that in common too. Robert often took Gretchen to his friend's summer cottage in the Laurentians. Isobel and Bernice joined them at least once. Jack remembered the photographs—everyone smiling and happy.

But yesterday, despite how hard he tried, nothing worked. Gretchen hadn't spoken or smiled. Except when he had retold the story when Prime Minister King had visited Dad at their cottage: *Remember that summer, Gretch? You were sixteen, maybe seventeen. Mr. King visited us, and there was the dance with the gramophone on the veranda. Remember Mother? Isobel had danced with Mr. King, and I think Margaret wanted to, but Dad wouldn't let her.* Jack had felt elated when he caught Gretchen's hint of a smile.

Jack unfolded himself, looked up and out over the car's dashboard towards the Bay, then over his shoulder to see if Boyle had arrived. No sign. He thought back to last night at the house. The call had come in around eight-thirty. Cora had just put Bob to bed. It had been Dad asking if Gretchen was with them. She had gone for a walk, according to Dad, but hadn't returned. He had sounded unusually distressed. Jack had driven over as soon as he hung up. When he'd arrived, Jack remembered his dad's face: pale, drawn, and how his hands shook. Mother had been calm, reserved. Like Margaret. But Margaret, as usual was bossy. She had informed them that Gretchen's coat and handbag were gone from her room. That was all that was missing, according to Margaret, but she had to add that Gretchen's room was a mess. Jack was always annoyed by Margaret's antics. It was draining. Over the past few years, there has been animosity between them, more so since he bought the store. Likely, it was because Margaret knew that Dad had put up the money for the down payment. But he reminded himself that Margaret had some redeeming qualities —how she loved her nieces and nephews, for instance, including his boys. She adored them. The children felt the same way. Aunt Margaret was much loved.

He thought back again to last night, when Margaret stated it was pointless to call Gretchen's friends, who had all moved away. But he had telephoned the Baines, the Crawfords, and the Murphys anyway. He spoke to the mothers. All had inquired about

Gretchen's health. None had seen her. Dad had suggested calling Gretchen's physician, Stott, until Margaret had informed them that Doctor Stott was in Toronto for a conference. It was then that Jack had started to feel the familiar wave of anxiety. He had wanted a drink badly. He'd begun to perspire profusely. It was a relief when Margaret had left to put Heather and Hugh to bed, and Mother followed.

Dad had come to his rescue. Both he and Dad had gone to the front parlour, but before sitting down, Dad had put his finger to his lips and then left the room. Jack heard his footsteps as he went down the hall, then the creak of the door to the cellar. He had returned a few minutes later with a bottle of whiskey and two tumblers—*from your mother's medicinal stash,* he'd said when handing Jack the bottle and two glasses. Jack filled up both and drained his, while Dad took one sip before putting his glass on the table. Jack had poured himself another. They sat like that for a while.

He had spoken first, suggesting they call Boyle. Dad had nodded in agreement. Jack recalled the conversation: *Operator? Good evening... Chief Boyle please, number one-six-one. Thank you. Hello Boyle? Yes, Jack Kastner here. It is about Gretchen...my father and I are concerned—yes, I'm with him at the house. She left around seven this evening, and she's not back...yes...by herself left with her coat and handbag—said she was going to friends... No, she didn't mention who with... Fine. Thank you. See you shortly.*

After Jack had hung up the telephone, they sat in silence until he had wondered aloud if they should call Robert. Dad had become agitated at the suggestion: *No. I don't want to call him. Robert has brought nothing but grief to your sister. Having her come here to Wiarton, so your sister can file for divorce, so that he will be free to remarry—marry the woman in Montreal. It's ludicrous... His lawyer has already started the process; he's contacted Snider... But I don't want to talk about it anymore. I want to find your sister...*

The sharp knock at the door had interrupted Dad's tirade. It had been Chief Boyle. Thank God for Boyle. He had felt reassured after they spoke. Maybe it had been Boyle's demeanour or his warmth. Or maybe it was because he was feeling vulnerable and out-of-control and felt relieved that someone else was taking charge. Boyle had been aware of Gretchen's situation. There were no secrets in Wiarton. He'd asked if Gretchen might have gone to Owen Sound to catch a train to Montreal, or if she might have gone to Toronto to visit her sister Isobel, or a school friend. Possibly, they had not thought of that. This had given Jack a sense of hope. *Don't worry, she'll turn up,* were Boyle's parting words. Then he left, taking his confidence with him.

Jack thought back to what had happened next—Dad dozing in his chair. He wasn't sure for how long, but he too had dozed off and then woke up with a start. He had looked at his watch—four thirty. Jack remembered that surge of fear—that feeling of anxiety he experienced in the early hours when everyone was asleep and daylight was vague. And the familiar scene that ran through his head again and again: How did I miss that turn? I couldn't stop... my toes crushed when I pushed the brake... crashing into the tree. Then, blackness. Then red.

Jack had found himself in the driveway of his house. He didn't remember how he got there but remembered looking at his watch—it had been five-fifty. He had gone in and woken up Cora, telling her they were still looking for Gretchen. *Not to worry; we'll find her. I'll be back soon.* Then he went into Paul's room. He told him he wouldn't be going to school that day. He kissed his forehead. He had wanted to hug him tight and not let go.

Jack got back to Hillcrest at ten past six. He found his dad asleep in his armchair. Jack had sat down and finished his father's whiskey. It was the clanking of pots and dishes a few minutes later that roused Dad. It was six thirty. Clemmie was getting breakfast ready. He remembered the comforting smell of fresh coffee, then the jarring sound of the telephone. *Jack? Boyle here. Meet me at the long dock at...* There had been a brief pause...*nine-thirty. We found what we think might be Gretchen's coat and handbag.* Boyle had hung up before Jack could ask any questions.

Jack driving a motorboat at Oliphant on Lake Huron, possibly on Victoria Day or Dominion Day [indicated by the Union Jack flag]. c. 1931 – 1935

CHAPTER THREE

# CHIEF BOYLE

B OYLE GLANCED AT HIS watch. It read nine twenty-five. It felt like the middle of the afternoon. The day was not going to get any easier. He looked in the rear view mirror and could see Hacking's car following several yards behind. Stott, typically the coroner for Wiarton, was apparently in Toronto; Hacking was the back-up. He was from the nearby town of Tara. Boyle had worked with Hacking a couple of times. He was a good man—well respected.

Boyle scanned the parking lot and spotted Jack's car near the Fish House. He could see Jack's outline behind the wheel. He pulled up to Jack's car, parking on the passenger side. Hacking pulled up beside him, leaving several feet between the police car and his own.

Boyle got out of his car slowly. He knocked lightly on the driver's-side window. Jack startled. Boyle noticed Jack's face first, then his clothes. His face was strained—pale and fearful. His suit looked creased and rumpled, as if he'd slept in it. But, most likely, Boyle thought, Jack hadn't slept much since he'd seen him and his father the night before. Poor chap. Boyle grimaced as he prepared for what he had to do next.

"Morning Jack." Boyle reached his hand towards Jack's as Jack got out of the car. Boyle left out "good" from his customary greeting—it was not a good morning for the Kastner family. "As I mentioned on the telephone this morning Mr. Kastner, a woman's coat and handbag were found sometime just after five this morning at the end of the long dock. What I didn't mention when we spoke is that after Macaulay, who found the items, telephoned me, I decided to call on Charles Hull to go to the dock. I was thinking that if the items were Gretchen's, Hull could help with the search. You probably know Hull—he's the chief of the fire brigade here in Wiarton." He noted Jack's nod. Boyle paused, then continued. "Macaulay had suggested that he and Hull go out onto the Bay to see if they could see anything. Apparently, they took the tug out." Boyle paused again, this time a few seconds longer. He cleared his throat. "They did find her, Jack. Sometime after six o'clock. They brought her... her back here and called me to come down." Boyle gestured towards the Fish House. The building was several yards from where they were standing. "We are quite certain it is Gretchen. I'm very sorry, Jack. I telephoned Doctor Hacking since Stott appears to be out of town. He met me at the station and followed me here." Boyle nodded towards Hacking, who was still sitting in his car.

Boyle paused, giving time for Jack to respond. He didn't. Boyle continued, "Doctor Hacking is here to examine her and complete... the paperwork. Now... are you able... can you... can you see Gretchen?" Boyle felt himself struggling with his words. His mouth felt as if it were filled with cotton batten. "You will be with the doc the whole time. You will also need to provide... details. If you don't feel up to it, Mr. Kastner, or can't, I understand. I could call your father."

"No. I can do it."

Boyle studied Jack's face. It had transformed in the last few seconds from a facade of defeat to one that was stiff and stone-like—stoic even. Boyle had learned from his years of police service that people's reaction to news of an unexpected death were unpredictable. Reactions ran the gamut. Often, it was those who showed the least emotion who took it the hardest. Jack was probably one.

God knows his family has had its share of strife. He had heard that Jack had lost an infant son a few years ago. And now this. Boyle looked over at Hacking's car. They made eye contact. The doctor got out of his car with his black bag in hand and walked towards them.

"Morning, Mr. Kastner. Roy Hacking from Tara. I know your father, Gideon, quite well. I wish we were meeting under different circumstances, son." Jack nodded as they shook hands. They stood for several seconds in awkward silence until Boyle waved toward the Fish House. The three walked towards the building, with Boyle leading the way. Upon opening the door and entering, Boyle felt his nostrils singe. The odour was powerful. The smell of damp wood and fish wrapped around them. Boyle found it oddly comforting. He had been in the Fish House a handful of times over the years, but not under this kind of circumstance. Jack and the doctor stood beside him. He followed Jack's eyes, which were fixed on the counter in front of them. On it were the coat and handbag Macaulay had found. Macaulay must have taken great care to fold up the coat like it was now, with the belt wrapped around the coat and the handbag propped neatly beside it. How odd they looked in this setting, Boyle thought. He looked toward Jack. He had not moved.

Jack spoke: "They are Gretchen's. The coat and handbag."

Boyle didn't respond. He wasn't sure what to say. They stood in a thick silence. It was broken by Macaulay who entered from outside. Boyle was certain Macaulay knew the doctor but decided to introduce him formally. Macaulay was a fixture in the Wiarton community. He had been fishing on the Bay for over fifty years. He was the current owner of the Fish House, which he'd taken over from Booth Fisheries a few years ago. Fishing was tough business these days, Boyle knew, but if anyone could make it work, it was Macaulay.

"Macaulay I'd like you to meet Doctor Hacking. He is acting as coroner today, filling in for Doctor Stott. Doctor Hacking, this is John Macaulay, owner of the Fish House. And Macaulay, you know Mr. Kastner, of course."

"Greetings, Mr. Kastner. And Doc." Macaulay nodded and took off his cap. Boyle noticed how Macaulay greeted Jack first. It was a sign of respect for a local. "She's in here." Macaulay walked over to the door behind the counter, gesturing for the doctor to enter. "We placed her on a table here Doc. We put a blanket on her. It's from one of my boats, so it's a bit damp. Sorry. It was the best we could do for her."

Boyle noticed how Macaulay's voice lowered when speaking about Gretchen. This morning, Boyle remembered how distraught Macaulay had been when he spoke about how they found Gretchen in the water. Gruff on the exterior, but Boyle knew that Macaulay had deep feelings for Wiarton's families, especially those like the Kastners.

"Thank you, Mr. Macaulay. You did a fine job." Hacking smiled at him as he entered with his black bag in hand. He shut the door quietly behind him.

The three men stood in silence. They could sense that the doctor was moving within the office from the sound of the cracking coming from the wooden floorboards. Then it went quiet. The silence felt oppressive. Boyle didn't know what to say. He looked over at Jack. His expression hadn't changed. Boyle wondered how Jack's parents would take the news. He looked at Macaulay who was staring at the floor. The silence and the smells of The Fish House were similar for the three of them, Boyle guessed, but not their thoughts. Boyle said a prayer for the Kastners. God give them strength.

Several minutes later, Hacking opened the door. "I'm ready for you, Jack."

Boyle exhaled. He looked over at Jack. "Ready?"

Jack nodded and led the way.

CHAPTER FOUR

# DICKIE'S SHADOW

Boyle followed Jack into the office. Macaulay stayed back; he said there wasn't enough room for four. He was right. The room felt claustrophobic despite the window. There were two desk chairs and a cabinet pushed against one wall. The table, in the middle of the room, was illuminated by a light that hung from the ceiling. It cast a distorted yellow circle on Gretchen, or what was presumably Gretchen, as Jack could only see an outline of what looked like a woman's body. She was covered with an Army-green wool blanket that Jack could tell was more than damp, despite what Macaulay had said—it was wet. He knew by the heavy, sourly sweet odour. It reminded him of the smell from his boys' wool mittens after they came in from playing in the snow and Cora hung them to dry by the kitchen stove.

The doctor spoke first: "I'd like you to identify the body, Jack. I'm sorry to put you in this position. It is a formality—I'm acting in the role of county coroner now for the Province of Ontario. It is something we are required to do. Are you all right to proceed?"

Jack nodded. This felt familiar. Like déjà vu, but not. It was over twelve years ago that Richard had died. Sweet baby Richard—Dickie they had called him. It was at the hospital in London: different doctor, similar words.

He watched Hacking bend over and pull the blanket back. Jack looked at her face. Her skin was translucent. She looked strangely at peace, beautiful but empty and colourless at the same time. He cleared his throat. "It is Gretchen. It's my sister—Gretchen Kastner." The room suddenly felt far away. He felt, rather than heard, a high-pitched ringing sound in his ears. It was interrupted by Doctor Hacking speaking. Yet his voice was distant, as if he were talking to someone else in another room.

"Thank you, Jack." Doctor Hacking placed the blanket back over Gretchen's face. "After completing the examination, it appears your sister drowned. She likely had been in the water for a few hours, but no more than twelve, based on the condition of her body. This seems to be in line with what Chief Boyle has told me. My guess is that she swam into the Bay with the intent of self-inflicted drowning. I understand that she was a strong swimmer, so I can find no other explanation. I am sorry Jack, sorry for your loss, for your family."

The words echoed. Words from twelve years ago that played over and over in his head: *I am sorry for your loss. Very sorry for your family, your wife, and your older son.* Jack suddenly felt like he couldn't breathe—it felt as if his lungs didn't have enough air.

"Jack, are you all right? I have some paperwork to complete and need answers to a few questions from next of kin, but we can do this tomorrow." Hacking paused. "Jack?" He studied Jack closely and then pulled up one of the chairs, placing it several feet from the table. He motioned for Jack to sit down.

Jack wasn't sure how long Hacking had been waiting for an answer. He felt disoriented, as if he were a spectator to the events taking place in the room, looking down from above. He thought he heard himself speak, "Now." He saw himself standing upright.

The doctor nodded. He reached into his black bag and pulled out a form. Jack recognized it as a death certificate. It looked the same as when Dickie died. Jack thought back to the hospital—after the car accident at Victoria Hospital. We were half-way to Wiarton, he remembered; we only had three hours to go. It was for a short vacation, I'd told Cora—yet it wasn't. She knew. We had lost almost everything two weeks earlier. I'd lost father's money—the money from the property in Detroit. The Ford stock had been doing so well—then the crash. Strange, I had never thought of it before—one crash leading to another. The tree. The car. The doctors trying to save him. A fractured skull was what had killed him. That was what Doctor Dakins had written on Dickie's death certificate. The same one that Hacking is looking at now.

"Gretchen was born here in Wiarton?" Hacking asked looking expectantly at Jack. Waiting.

"Yes, here in Wiarton."

Jack remembered, as if it were yesterday, Doctor Dakins, the doctor at the London hospital, asking the same question: *Where was Richard born?*

Jack: *He was born in Detroit, Michigan. I was running a business there, and then we were driving back... back home.*

Hacking: "Gretchen's date of birth?"

"September 1, 1907."

Dakins: *When was your son born, Mr. Kastner?*

Jack: *July 12, 1928.* Jack remembered that it was a Thursday and that their neighbour, in the upstairs apartment, had watched Paul while he and Cora went to the hospital. Paul was three years old. Soon to be a big brother.

Hacking: "Where was your father's birthplace—Gideon's birthplace?"

Jack: "Our father was born in Sebringville, Ontario. He was one of ten brothers and two sisters."

Dakins: *And your birth date, Mr. Kastner?*

Jack: *I was born in Ontario. Wiarton, Ontario.*

Hacking: "And your mother's maiden name and birthplace?"

Jack: "It's Symon. Annie Symon. She was born in Ontario—I can't think of the city right now."

Hacking: "Not to worry, Jack. I'll write Ontario. That should suffice."

Dakins: *And your wife's name and birthplace, Mr. Kastner?*

Jack: *Anne Cora Gardner. She was born in Mount Forest, Ontario.* Jack thought back to Cora when they first had met, how she was the youngest of five girls and the prettiest by far.

Hacking: "And what is the name of Gretchen's husband?"

Jack: "Robert Doull. He is responsible... for this." Jack waved his hand towards Gretchen's body. Hacking didn't respond. He began filling in the remaining details on his own:

> PERSON GIVING INFORMATION: Jack Kastner; ADDRESS: Wiarton, Ontario; RELATIONSHIP TO DECEASED: brother; CAUSE OF DEATH: suicide by drowning; CONTRIBUTORY FACTORS: none; DATE OF DEATH: Hacking hesitated here. Likely it was May 27, last evening but he had to go by when the body was found. He wrote, May 28, 1941.

Jack looked at the Doctor Hacking as he stooped over the table filling in the rest of the form's blanks. He remembered Dickie's doctor doing the same thing. Jack knew the details of Dickie's death certificate by heart.

> PERSON GIVING INFORMATION: Jack Kastner; ADDRESS: Detroit; RELATIONSHIP TO DECEASED: father; CAUSE OF DEATH: fracture of skull with contusions of brain; CONTRIBUTORY FACTORS: car driven by father left the road and crashed into a tree; DATE OF DEATH: November 12, 1929.

"Thank you, Jack. I am sure this was difficult. Again, I am sorry son for your loss. Please give my condolences to your father and mother. My thoughts and prayers are with your family." Hacking's tone was fatherly. He held onto Jack's arm for a few seconds, then turned away, placing the form and his pen in his doctor's bag.

Jack felt as if he were going to be sick. The room began to swirl. His ears were ringing, louder than before. He walked out of the room, brushed past Boyle, past the counter with Gretchen's coat and handbag, and out the front door. He went to the side of the building, crouched down, and put his head in his hands.

What do I do now? How do I tell Dad and Mother about another loss? A child has died—not a grandchild, but their child. He remembered back to when Richard died and the telegram he had sent to his father:

> Car accident in London STOP Cora severely injured Paul has broken arm STOP Richard died STOP Please come at once STOP Victoria Hospital, London STOP.

Now he had to tell his parents about another tragedy, but this time face-to-face.

Hillcrest, when it was occupied by the first owners, the Kyle family. Naming homes in the Victorian era was common. "Hillcrest" derives from its location—on a hill, overlooking town. c. 1880

CHAPTER FIVE

# HILLCREST

HILLCREST SITS AT THE corner of Gould and Mary streets in Wiarton. She is built of buff brick and local limestone with five bedrooms, a library, two kitchens, a music room (sometimes used as a courting parlour), a front parlour, a dining room, and two chimneys. The taller chimney has a letter "H" for Hillcrest embedded within her brickwork. She has housed three families so far: the Kyles, the Acres, and the Kastners. Hillcrest is proud of the fact that not only does she provide her families with shelter and warmth, but she is also a keeper of their stories.

Jack's car pulls into her gravel driveway. He gets out, closes the door gently, and walks towards the back entrance. The back door leads to the summer kitchen. It's not typically used by family members except by Jack when he visits and when he and Margaret used to keep chickens in the hen house in the backyard. Usually it's the domestic staff going to and fro, but happily for Hillcrest, the Kastner grandchildren now pass through to get to their bicycles, pushchairs, and toys that have found a home there.

Jack enters the kitchen, where Clemmie, the cook who lives upstairs, is washing the breakfast dishes. Her sleeves are rolled up past her elbows and her white apron is damp with dishwater. Hugh and Heather are nearby, on the floor, playing with Hugh's toy trains. Clemmie looks up and notes Jack's face, then looks down and bites her lip. Jack nods and walks into the dining room, where he finds Gideon, Margaret, and Annie sitting at the table drinking coffee.

The dining room is the hub of Hillcrest—over the years, it has held at least four to six family members twice a day, every day, and more now with the grandchildren. The three look up expectantly as Jack enters. The room feels anxious despite the sounds from the kitchen—the clacking of Clemmie stacking dishes and screeches of delight from Heather as she plays with her brother.

Jack begins speaking, "Gretchen drowned. She drowned in the Bay last night or early this morning. Gretchen's coat and handbag were found at the end of the long dock by Macaulay." He pauses. Moaning sounds can be heard from Annie and Margaret. Gideon is silent.

"I met Chief Boyle and Doctor Hacking at the dock. I saw her. Macaulay and Hull brought her in on a boat." Jack reaches for a handkerchief in his pocket and mops his brow. "She is not suffering any longer. May she rest in peace."

Gideon begins to speak. Annie starts crying, as does Margaret. The room vibrates with distraught energy. It sounds as if everyone is speaking, shouting, or crying all at once. No one is listening except for Hillcrest.

Clemmie enters the dining room, stands by the door, and then disappears. The adults weep while the children continue to play. The house expands in an effort to cocoon her family, hold them together, and soothe their suffering.

Margaret's voice rises above the rest: "It's Robert's fault. Why did he ask for a divorce? Why did he want Gretchen to move back here?"

"Shh, Margaret, the children will hear you." Now, it's Annie speaking.

"I don't understand how this could have happened. She seemed to be getting better. She told me two days ago how she was looking forward to moving into the Paterson house. We shouldn't have let her go out for a walk last night in her state. She seemed upset after she came back from the car ride. Jack, why did you take her out? It made her worse. What did you say to her?"

"Margaret", Annie says, "it's not Jack's fault. I was there. He was trying to cheer her up. We all were. Gretchen was the same as she's been since she's been home." Annie walks over to Margaret and puts her arms around her. Margaret cries.

Clemmie re-enters the dining room, composed, with a bottle of Seagram's. She had been to the cellar. She puts the full bottle of whiskey on the table, goes to the sideboard, and takes out four glasses and places them beside the bottle. "I'll go to the children. I won't say anything about their Mum."

"Thank you, Clemmie." Jack gives her a wan smile. He goes to the table and opens the bottle. It makes a "crack" sound as the seal breaks. He fills each glass halfway.

Hillcrest can hear clinking sounds made by glass on glass—the only audible sound. Even the children are suddenly quiet. Jack offers a drink to his mother first. Annie takes the glass. She has never seen Annie drink within her walls. Jack passes a glass to Gideon, then Margaret. Margaret and Annie continue to cry. Gideon stares ahead. Jack empties his drink first. He fills his glass again.

The family sits together for what feels like a long time, their grief binding them together. Gideon breaks the silence: "We need to contact your sisters and the reverend. And someone will need to call Robert."

"I'll call Bernice and Isobel. They'll likely come tomorrow, if not tonight," Margaret says.

Jack speaks after Margaret: "I can call Robert. I'll go to the store and call him from there since, Margaret, you'll need to use the telephone here at the house to make the calls."

"I'll go with you," Gideon says, and then he begins to cry. No one had ever seen Gideon cry, not even when Dickie died.

Hillcrest shifts her limestone footings in response to the loss within her family, and to their pain. It is a new season.

CHAPTER SIX

# DOCTOR STOTT

THE TELEPHONE RINGS ABRUPTLY. Sydney sighs. He is nearing the bottom of his mail pile. He had returned last evening from the three-day conference in Toronto, exhausted. Scheduling patients for today was a mistake, he realizes. A glance at his watch tells him he has fifteen minutes until his first appointment. He decides to answer the telephone and picks up the earpiece: "Doctor Stott here."

"Sydney? It is Doctor Roy Hacking here—from Tara. I'm glad you are back from Toronto."

Sydney knew Hacking. The circle of doctors in the county was small, and Hacking was well liked by the group, including by Sydney. It was not uncommon within their enclave that the older doctors, like Hacking, used first names when speaking to the younger doctors.

"Good morning, Doctor Hacking. What can I do for you?"

"Sydney, I am afraid I have bad news to share. Your patient, Gretchen Kastner—Gretchen Doull I should say, is dead. She drowned in the Bay last night. Unfortunately, it was suicide. I've just returned to my office from The Fish House at the long dock with Chief Boyle and Jack Kastner. Boyle called me up early this morning to fill in as coroner since he couldn't get a hold of you. He thought you were still in Toronto. Gretchen went missing last evening, and Macaulay found her, along with Hull, early this morning. She was in the Bay. I examined the body: fluid in her lungs, skin macerations on her extremities, and evidence of froth in her nose and mouth cavities. All indicators suggest she suffered from asphyxia, most definitely caused by drowning. My guess is that she may have taken a dose of barbiturates before swimming out into the Bay. I'm not sure. But either way, the cause of death was drowning. Self-inflicted drowning." There was a pause.

Sydney felt a surge of adrenaline shoot through his body. Gretchen was his first patient to commit suicide. Thoughts raced through his head, including how Gretchen presented to him six weeks ago: poised, soft-spoken, suffering from insomnia and depression. His hands began to shake.

"Sydney? Are you still there?"

"Yes. Sorry, I'm just... She seemed to be improving. She was, I thought, getting better."

"Very distressing, I know. Difficult too for the Kastner family. They have had their share of challenges. This is another tragedy for them. But don't blame yourself, son. I understand how disconcerting it is to lose a patient, but it is not your fault. I am finishing up the death certificate today and will forward it to the Registrar General. Likewise, I will send you the summary notes for her file. And, as I said before, don't blame yourself. I am here if you need anything."

Sydney heard the click on Hacking's end. He placed the telephone earpiece back in its cradle, his hands still shaking.

I never thought it would come to this. Maybe if I hadn't gone to Toronto for that conference... If only I had been here. He thought back to the last time he saw Gretchen. It was twelve days ago—Thursday, May 15. She had seemed better, not good, but improving. She spoke of how she was going to be moving into her own house with Heather and Hugh, across the street from her parents. She seemed to be looking forward to it. He could tell by her voice. It had broken out of its usual monotone. He had sensed restrained excitement. Progress he had thought. He remembered the first visit when Gretchen's sister Margaret had brought her in. Margaret had appeared exasperated. *We don't know what to do with her Doctor Stott. She doesn't sleep or eat much, and she walks alone for hours. She appears... not herself.* Gretchen's father, Gideon had followed up with a telephone call the next day urging him to call Gretchen's doctor in Montreal—a Doctor Burns.

Sydney's diagnosis of Gretchen, even before he had spoken to Burns, was depressed mood and insomnia, along with symptoms and behaviours consistent with anorexia nervosa. He had recently read about anorexia in the American Medical Association's journal. A colleague who he had gone to school with at University of Toronto, Ray Farquharson, co-wrote an article that described the phenomenon of patients losing weight by restricting food intake. Farquharson's findings suggested weight loss was intentional and consistent with emotional distress rather than physiological factors including lack of appetite. Sydney thought it consistent with Gretchen's symptoms. He was very familiar with emotional disturbances, having witnessed several during the First World War while he served. It was why he went to medical school—to learn to treat the sick and heal their pain. Yet Gretchen's pain was the kind that medical school didn't teach how to heal. But Farquharson's article had provided insight into at least one of her conditions. It had been considerably more helpful than Gretchen's former doctor in Montreal, Burns. He had called Burns more out of courtesy to Gretchen's father, but he had been curious about what Burns' diagnosis was.

Sydney had determined early in their conversation that Burns was old-school. Burns shared how he had diagnosed Gretchen with hysteria and subsequently prescribed bed rest and Veronal for sleep. Hysteria, Sydney remembered from his medical school textbooks, was a diagnosis dating back to the Greeks, yet Freud had pushed it further, theorizing that it was a female-only disease triggered by psychological scars and trauma. Freud claimed it was associated with a variety of symptoms, mostly physical, along with behaviours described as "dejection of spirits." The hysteria diagnosis was falling out of favour, but some doctors, like Burns, continued to diagnose female patients with the so-called disease, prescribing bed rest and often sleeping aids.

Sydney remembered how he had discussed with Gretchen that Veronal was not a long-term solution. But he had felt perplexed about a course of treatment. What would have been the best way to treat her? He had considered several options. One was the new method used for severe cases of depression—electric convulsive therapy. But he had quickly ruled that out—it was experimental and risky. Another was insulin therapy, a procedure to shock the system into a coma. It was initially used for schizophrenic patients, but some doctors claimed it was effective for severely depressed patients. But the data on its efficacy was inconclusive. Another option he had considered was to send her to a psychiatrist at one of the new clinics. There was one in Toronto. Psychiatric therapy, however, was still new with scant published data on its effectiveness, and, from what Sydney had surmised, it was time-consuming. Then, there was the outdated course of action—the "rest cure," as Burns had suggested. There were sleeping aids too, like Veronal, which were frequently prescribed regardless of whether patients were following a rest regime or not.

Stott wasn't convinced that Veronal or any other barbiturates were effective, even in the short term. He found that symptoms usually reappeared, often worse than before, once patients stopped taking the drug. If anything, Sydney had observed, it was the passage of time that healed. But he had felt a sense of urgency with Gretchen, a sense of desperation every time he saw her.

Damn. I should have done something. I am sorry Gretchen, that I couldn't help you. I let you down. I let your family down.

Sydney shakes his head, takes a deep breath, and stands up in preparation for his next patient.

Gretchen will forever haunt him.

Gideon Litt Kastner. c. 1930

CHAPTER SEVEN

# GIDEON

GIDEON SITS ACROSS FROM Jack. The space is cramped; their knees graze under the table that Jack uses as a desk. They are in the backroom of Kastner Menswear Store. Selling suits is not a business Gideon would have chosen for Jack, but it was the only option last year when Jack needed a job. He had been running out of vocation choices. Gideon thought back to what brought Jack and him to this point. It had been a long journey, but the catalyst was when they both lost their jobs at the Wiarton Furniture Factory five years ago. He had been a founder of the company, and as a major shareholder and board-appointed general manager, he was able to give Jack a job as the company's bookkeeper. But this caused considerable tension and ultimately led to a power struggle among the shareholders. Eventually, both he and Jack were asked to leave. Seventy-one at the time, Gideon could retire, but Jack could not; he had a young family to support.

Gideon remembered how he had used his contacts in the lumber industry to help Jack find another job—a sales manager position at the Beach Furniture Factory in Cornwall. The job had been short-lived. Gideon never got the full story, but within one year, Jack was back in Wiarton. It is not all his fault, Gideon thought, given what Jack has been through with the accident, losing the baby, and Cora's surgeries. Putting up the money to help Jack buy the store seemed like a reasonable investment at the time, but with the onset of the War, it hadn't turned out that way. And now this. I have lost my Gretchen. My beautiful, beautiful daughter. How happy she was as a child and teenager—intelligent, with a quick wit and kind heart. My dear, beloved Gretchen.

"Would you like a drink, Dad?" Jack stands at the table, holding a half-full bottle of whiskey in one hand and two glasses in the other.

Gideon turns his attention back to Jack. He wonders where Jack keeps his alcohol stash. "No, thanks son. I'll wait until after we call Robert." Gideon senses Jack's concern. It is the furrowed brow visible over Jack's eyeglasses that gives it away. "I'm okay son. Really."

Jack nods, puts the two tumblers on the table, fills his near the top, places the bottle on the table, and sits down. Jack takes one sip, then another.

On the drive over they had decided that Jack would be the one to call Robert. Gideon had offered, but Jack insisted. Just as well thought Gideon, I might say something I will regret. He thought back to when he first learned of Robert's strategy for divorcing Gretchen. His lawyer, Snider, had told him that it was likely that Robert planned to leverage Ontario's Divorce Act, which had passed in 1930. The Act, according to Snider, allowed a spouse who was residing in Ontario and who had been separated for two years, to apply for divorce. It would explain why Gretchen had returned to Wiarton with the children. Robert, from what he could gather, had wanted Gretchen to initiate the divorce here.

Ontario's judicial law was very much in Robert's favour, Snider had told him. Divorce was next to impossible in Quebec, where Gretchen and Robert had been living since they married. Robert would have had to place a "notice of intent" in the Canadian Gazette and two of the same in local newspapers outlining his wish to divorce. Next, he'd have to submit his petition and hope he was granted a divorce by the Crown, nullifying the marriage. The likelihood of being granted a divorce following this route was slim. It was no wonder that Robert wanted Gretchen to return to Wiarton. Gideon remembers how furious he was when he found out. Robert was a tremendous disappointment. He liked him when he and Gretchen first married. Robert was an upstanding, intelligent young man, university-educated with an engineering degree. And from a good family. Annie even approved—Robert's parents were Presbyterians, as her parents were. It had seemed a perfect match.

"Dad… Dad? I think we should call Robert now. It is just about lunchtime. Robert will likely still be in the office."

That was another thing, Gideon had been proud of Robert's job. He worked at Dominion Engineering Works as a mechanical engineer in Montreal. It was an important position and provided a good income. Yet Dominion was where Robert had met Nina, the woman he wanted to marry. She was a secretary there. Gideon shook his head, focusing his attention back on Jack. "Yes, son. I agree. Do you have Doull's number?"

"I have it here." Jack gets up, goes to the file cabinet, opens the top drawer, and pulls out an address book. He brings it back to the table, flips through the small folio and lays it open on the table. "Ready?"

Gideon nods.

After picking up the telephone's earpiece, Jack takes an audible deep breath. Gideon watches him dial '0' with his other hand. He noticed it was shaking, slightly.

"Operator? I'd like to place a long distance call to Montreal, Quebec, to Robert Doull." Jack looks at the phone book. "At Dominion Engineering—number 72-R-25." Jack looks at Gideon and raises his eyebrows. Gideon can hear the clicking noises.

"Thank you, operator. Yes. Robert Doull at Dominion Engineering—number again is 72-R-25. This is Jack Kastner calling from Wiarton, Ontario. It is an urgent call." He turns to look at Gideon covering the earpiece, "She is putting me through Dad."

They wait. Jack leans forward slightly over the table, the phone's earpiece still held up to his ear. Gideon notices how Jack's shoulders are raised and the faint band of sweat on his forehead.

"Robert? Yes…hello. It is Jack Kastner here. I am calling from Wiarton. Gideon is here with me. I am afraid we have some bad news. It is about Gretchen." Jack clears his throat. His voice gets louder. "She is dead, Robert. I am sorry." Jack pauses tilting the earpiece towards Gideon, but Gideon can't make out any words. "The children are fine. Yes, well… Gretchen had gone for a walk last night after dinner to visit some friends. She apparently went to the long dock. Yes, it's the dock that's further from town… Yes past Blue Water Park. She must have gone into the water sometime before midnight and swam out. She drowned… No… No. I don't think so… The coroner ruled it as suicide. I met with him this morning at the dock. They found her body around six this morning." Jack listens, nods his head then looks at Gideon.

"I know, I know. But as you are aware, Robert, she hasn't been well and has been depressed since she's been back in Wiarton. There has not been much improvement. She had been in Doctor Stott's care." Jack stops talking, looks at Gideon, and tilts the earpiece again towards him. Gideon can hear Robert's voice—his words are unclear, but his voice sounds distressed.

"Margaret and my mother are with the children. They are all right. We have not told them yet. Yes, Dad and I are here at the store. We are planning to have the funeral this Friday." Jack pauses, then looks at Gideon, raising his eyebrows. "Father can't speak right now."

Gideon nods.

"No, I don't think so. We can discuss the children's care when you come to Wiarton for the funeral. Yes, and don't worry; they are fine. You'll drive then? All right. We will see you tomorrow. I will tell them… See you then." Jack puts the earpiece back in its cradle. He lets out a loud sigh and reaches for the whiskey bottle and pours himself another drink, then holds the bottle over Gideon's glass.

Gideon shakes his head. "How did Robert take it?"

"He was distressed—he asked if it was an accident of some sort. Robert seemed to have a difficult time grasping that it was suicide." Jack stopped. He picked up his glass and finished his drink, then poured another until the glass was half full. "He also wanted to speak with you, but I thought it best that you speak in person when he comes for the funeral. He was concerned about Hugh and Heather and wanted me to tell them both that he would be here soon. He also said something about taking them back with him to Montreal after the funeral. There is no doubt that he was upset."

"I don't think that is going to happen. The children are staying here with family."

Jack picks up his glass and finishes his drink. He reaches into his pocket for his handkerchief, takes off his glasses, and wipes his brow, then one eye and the other. "I agree with you, Dad, but Robert is their father. He is family."

Gideon looks at Jack's red-rimmed eyes and tired face. He puts his arm on Jack's arm, patting it lightly. He thinks of Gretchen. I will miss you, my dear child. He holds his head down, saying a silent prayer for Gretchen and Jack.

CHAPTER EIGHT

# MABEL

IT IS AN HOUR UNTIL press time. Mabel looks at the clock and then back again to the Doull story on her desk. She had been struggling with the headline. The article had arrived at her desk half an hour ago with the headline "Suicide of Mrs. Doull on Wednesday." She had first changed it to "Death of Mrs. Doull on Wednesday," then "Unexpected Death of Mrs. Doull," and back again to the original headline. Mabel reads the three again and then writes, "Tragic Death of Mrs. Doull on Wednesday." That is it. It captures the story for what it is—a horrendous tragedy for the Kastner family and for the two children Mrs. Doull leaves behind. Mabel thinks how devastated Gideon and Annie Kastner must be. She draws a line through the other headlines and circles "Tragic Death of Mrs. Doull on Wednesday" with her pen.

Mabel is editor and publisher of The Canadian Echo, the weekly newspaper for Wiarton. She had taken over the paper five years ago after the death of her husband. She is one of the very few female newspaper editors in the country. For the few women who do work in the industry, the majority are relegated to writing women's interest columns. An even smaller number might work as editors of the social pages, which is what Mabel did before her husband died. Though petite, at just over five feet, Mabel is a powerhouse—an experienced journalist, editor, and skilled writer with a thick skin. The latter comes in handy. Not all staff at the *Echo* like Mabel in her editor role, nor does the reading public. Some appear to have preferred her late husband. But criticism doesn't faze Mabel one bit. She is passionate about her job. Her primary objective is to bring readers authentic, accurate journalism. Mabel believes the community newspaper serves as an archive—a record of a town's unique history. She said as much in this week's editorial titled "The Press and Local History." She wrote what she believed: "Few people as they read their weekly newspaper know that they are reading perhaps the only contemporary history of their community... the old fyles [files] of a newspaper are, from a historical standpoint, of incalculable worth."

After circling her new headline, Mabel rereads the article:

> TRAGIC DEATH OF MRS. DOULL ON WEDNESDAY
> A tragedy which stirred the town as it has seldom been stirred before occurred on Tuesday night when Mrs Gretchen Kastner Doull was drowned in Wiarton Bay. Mrs. Doull who was married in 1929 had been living in Montreal until a few weeks ago when she returned home with her two children. She had taken the Paterson house and had started to move in. On Tuesday night she had gone out and when she hadn't returned home later in the evening the family became worried and telephoned several friends in hope of locating her. Towards morning her coat and purse were discovered on the long dock. Chief Boyle was notified and he and Mr. Chas. Hull went on Wednesday to try to the waterfront to try and locate the body. Shortly it was recovered from the foot of the long dock. Mrs. Doull has been in poor health and terribly depressed since returning home.
>
> She is survived by her husband Robert Doull of Montreal, her two children, Hugh aged six and Heather, 13 months: her grief-stricken parents, Mr. and Mrs. Gideon Kastner; a brother John Kastner, of Wiarton, and three sisters: (Margaret) Mrs C. Mills, of Wiarton; (Bernice) Mrs. W Tuer, of St. Thomas, and (Isobel) Mrs. D'Arcy MacMahon, of Toronto. The funeral will be a private one on Friday afternoon at one o'clock.

Mabel signs the bottom of the article's page to indicate it's ready for press, then writes FRONT PAGE above the headline. She lets out a sigh. Strangely, she's gripped by a feeling of déjà vu. It was the words she just read in the article that were the trigger.

Mabel gets up and walks over to her bookshelf, where there are neat piles of newspapers from major cities that include Toronto, Montreal, and New York. She typically reads most, keeping two months' worth of each before discarding them. Mabel pulls out the New York Times pile and goes back to her desk. She scans through several of the back copies until she finds the two articles she is looking for. She reads the first article dated April 3: VIRGINIA WOOLF BELIEVED DEAD and skims the article:

> Mrs. Woolf... went for a walk last Friday ...and it is thought she has been drowned. Her body, however, has not been recovered. It was reported her hat and cane had been found on the bank of the Ouse River. Mrs. Woolf had been ill for some time.

She turns to the next one, dated April 19, and reads the headline: MRS. WOOLF'S BODY FOUND. VERDICT OF DROWNING IS RETURNED IN DROWNING OF NOVELIST. The article describes how Woolf's husband testified that "Mrs. Woolf had been depressed for a considerable length of time."

Mabel was struck by the similarities of the descriptions: both suffering from depression; going for a walk; personal effects found by a body of water; and suicide by drowning. Another coincidence was the date of Woolf's suicide—March 28. Two months to the day that Gretchen's body was found. How very odd.

Depression is devastating, she thinks, for everyone: families, spouses, and children. She slowly folds up both newspapers, puts them in the pile with the others, and returns them to the bookshelf. She picks up Gretchen's article from her desk and leaves her office. She walks briskly towards the print shop. It's time to get the press rolling. The news must go on.

64 FLOWERS OF HEAVEN

The Kastner siblings from left to right: Margaret, Jack,
Gretchen [front], Bernice and Isobel. c. 1915

CHAPTER NINE

# MARGARET

MARGARET HUNG THE EARPIECE back on the telephone. She is exhausted. It is the third time today that she has spoken with Reverend Sutherland about Gretchen's funeral. She had been on the telephone for the better part of the afternoon, arranging for the church service, contacting the pallbearers, and speaking with her sisters. Their cousins, Doug and Ken Symon, had agreed to be pallbearers, even though she had thought her brothers-in-law would be more appropriate. But Dad, for some reason, insisted that his two nephews, Doctor Stott and their family lawyer, Snider, as well as two other friends—Doctors Campbell and Hardman—take on the responsibility. She didn't agree, especially about Stott. But Margaret had acquiesced; now was not the time to argue.

Mother had been crying for most of the day—she was more than distraught. We all are, but Mother and Dad are understandably more so. Dad hasn't said much since he returned from the store with Jack. He must be in a state of shock.

She thought back to her telephone call with Isobel and Bernice. They were devastated. The three younger sisters were close growing up. Yet, with ten years between her and Gretchen, Margaret had always felt more like a mother figure to Gretchen and the other two. It was she who had been responsible for the three when they were at Branksome Hall in Toronto, while she attended St. Margaret's College School for Girls. It was less than a mile from Branksome, where the girls had also boarded. Dad and Mother thought it was the best arrangement since the girls were so young—they had felt better with her close by. Hers was a school that "prepared young women for university" according to the course catalogue as she remembered it. Except she didn't go to university afterwards like most of her classmates, but had attended a nursing program instead. Dad had wanted her to stay in Toronto to be near the girls. She remembered his words well. He was emphatic, stating it would be "practical and productive" to train as a nurse. Perhaps for some women, she thought, but not for her. Attending to the sick during the influenza epidemic had been enough. Watching the soldiers suffer and hearing their stories still haunts her. Her brief stint with her husband, Edward, was another reminder. He too had served and was never quite right afterwards, according to what his mother had said. Edward and she had lived together after their marriage for only a couple of years. That had been enough. She had done her duty.

Time for another drink.

Margaret walks into the dining room. Clemmie had left the bottle of whiskey on the dining room table on a tray, along with four clean glasses. She must have washed out the glasses from earlier that morning, likely guessing that this was the one and only time Mother would allow alcohol out in plain view. Thank God for Clemmie.

She pours herself a drink, then walks with it in hand towards the stairs. At the top of the staircase, rather than going to her room, she pauses and turns into Gretchen's. She closes the door behind her. The house is quiet until Margaret thinks she hears a sigh. Perhaps she imagines it.

She sips her drink and notices some photographs on Gretchen's dresser. There are several that are propped up against the mirror in a small stack. She picks them up and sits on the bed. She recognizes the one at the front, *Flowers of Heaven*. Margaret holds it closer and looks at the girls' faces. They look sombre. Likely, Margaret thinks, it's because the girls are posing in front of the cenotaph in Wiarton. She remembers that it had been erected a few years after World War I to memorialize the soldiers from Wiarton. That is probably how they gave the photograph its title—for the soldiers who died. Now Gretchen is with them—a flower in heaven.

Margaret looks at the next photograph—the girls are on a dock. It looks like the harbour near the long dock. Her stomach clenches. But there is Gretchen standing tall, with two friends sitting and three others below, including Bernice. Bernice was always part of the group, from what Margaret remembers, but it was Gretchen, even though she was younger than Bernice, who was the leader with her wry sense of humour and strong spirit. She studies her—this is our Gretchen, Margaret thinks—strong, confident, and happy.

She flips to the next one, *Freaks of Humanity*. Margaret chuckles. Why freaks, she wonders? There is Gretchen on top of a capstan with her arm around Bernice. She recognizes Margaret Baines, standing below Gretchen. Margaret was Gretchen's closest friend growing up. Gretchen was her maid of honour when Margaret married a few years ago. Margaret remembers how those girls used to talk incessantly. It used to irritate her to no end, especially when they were at the cottage. She sighs. "I am sorry Gretchen," she says out loud.

Margaret flips through to another two photographs: *Fools of High* and *Full of Hooch*. Margaret had never seen *Full of Hooch* before. The girls appear to be drunk. Margaret holds it up to get a better look. It looks like it was taken on Berford Street in broad daylight. It is very unlikely the girls were drunk. Prohibition was still on when the photograph was taken; most definitely, it was a prank. Margaret smiles. Likely, it was Gretchen's idea.

The last photograph from the pile is one of Margaret Baines and Gretchen at the cottage. Gretchen is sitting on a log, and

Margaret standing, resting her hands on Gretchen's shoulders. She looks closer at the photograph—it looks almost as if Margaret was trying to protect Gretchen. How odd. She'd never thought of that before—Gretchen needing protection.

Margaret finishes her drink and puts the photographs back on the dresser where she found them.

Gretchen, how very much you are loved—were loved. If only you knew, Margaret thought. A feeling of fear suddenly grips her—she thinks of Heather and Hugh. What will become of those children? Margaret thinks of Heather and how tightly she clings to her before she goes to sleep in her crib. She sometimes has to sit down with her, rocking her until she falls asleep. And then there's Hugh. At six, he puts on a brave face, but he lets her rub his back before he goes to bed, wash his hair, and help him brush his teeth. In the last couple of weeks, she has noticed how he follows her around the house. Clemmie told her how he asks, "Where's Aunt Margaret?" when she is out of sight. Poor little ones—what will happen to them, she wonders?

Jack had told her that Robert had said on the telephone that he planned to bring the children back to Montreal with him after the funeral.

I will talk with Robert and talk some sense into him. He must know what is best for the children. They belong here, where I can care for them.

She picks up her glass and leaves the room, closing the door quietly behind her.

Gretchen [second from right] and friends in front of Wiarton's war memorial. c. 1922 –1924

Freaks of Humanity. Gretchen [top left], her sister
Bernice [top centre] and friends. c. 1922–1924

Gretchen, [centre] her friends and sister Bernice [lower left] at a dock on Colpoy's Bay. c. 1922 –1924

CHAPTER TEN

# GRETCHEN

The Canadian Echo
VOL. 61—NUMBER 51
WIARTON, ONT.,
THURSDAY, JUNE 5, 1941

Funeral of the Late Mrs. R. Doull [page one]
The funeral of the late Mrs. Robert Doull was held on Friday [May 30] afternoon from the home of her father, Mr. Gideon Kastner and the rooms were filled with beautiful floral tributes, a silent tribute of sympathy. Rev. Wm. Sutherland had charge of the service and read the 23rd Psalm and other passages of comfort from the Scripture. He spoke of the Father's love and care for the child and said the same care and love was extended to the one suffering from neurasthenia who has become as a child. He quoted the passage "Like as a father pitieth his children, so that the Lord pitieth them that fear him." The pall-bearers were two cousins, Messrs. Douglas and Kenneth Symon, Dr. S.J. Stott, Dr. E.L. Hardman, Dr. A..M Campbell and L.H. Snider. Interment was made in Bayview Cemetery.

PSALM 23 The Lord is my shepherd; I shall not want.

He maketh me to lie down in green pastures: he leadeth me beside the still waters.

He restoreth my soul: he leadeth me in the paths of righteousness for his name's sake.

Yea, though I walk through the valley of the shadow of death, I will fear no evil: for thou art with me; thy rod and thy staff they comfort me.

Thou preparest a table before me in the presence of mine enemies: thou anointest my head with oil; my cup runneth over.

Surely goodness and mercy shall follow me all the days of my life: and I will dwell in the house of the Lord forever.

# EPILOGUE

PAUL KASTNER (1927 – 2018)
Paul tried to enlist towards the end of World War II, at the age of seventeen, but was unsuccessful due to his age. Shortly after, Paul ended up at the University of Manitoba, where he enrolled in the school of journalism. After two years, Paul left the program to pursue a job as a newspaper reporter, which eventually led him to a career in public relations. In 1959, he married Maxine Wamsley; they had a daughter two years later. Paul's job brought the family to various locales, including the United States. He and Maxine returned to the Oliphant area to live full-time in 1989. Their home was a short distance from the Kastner family cottage. Paul died at the age of ninety-one. He is remembered for his numerous contributions to the Wiarton community, including the founding of the William Wilfred Campbell Poetry & Arts Festival.

Paul was fourteen-years old when Gretchen died. He and his younger brother Bob were two of the few family members who saw Gretchen just prior to her death. When I met Paul in 2016, he recounted the car ride that he, his dad [Jack], mum [Anne (Cora)], grandmother [Annie], and Gretchen went on the afternoon preceding Gretchen's death. Paul remembered how sad Gretchen was that afternoon. He said it would haunt him forever. Paul also shared snippets of stories about Gretchen that he recalled overhearing during his childhood. One was about how Margaret used to visit Gretchen and Robert, apparently frequently, when they were living in Montreal. Paul remembered hearing that the visits had caused "problems" between Gretchen and Robert. He never learned what the problems were.

JOHN WILLIAM [JACK] KASTNER (1900 – 1953)
Jack continued operating his menswear store until his death. He died from cirrhosis of the liver, likely caused by the high levels of alcohol Jack reportedly consumed. Jack's obituary in *The Wiarton Echo* stated his death was "unexpected."

Jack seemed to have an entrepreneurial drive based on his various business ventures. Most were likely funded by Gideon. Jack first worked in the lumber business (including logging camps) for his dad after public school, and then, when he moved to Detroit, Michigan, in 1927, he started J. W. Kastner Co. & General Contractors. He located his office in a newly constructed office tower, the Maccabees Building, in downtown Detroit on Woodward Avenue. While there, Jack also owned a car wash business with a business partner, Moses Hassen, called "Hassen's Consolidated Auto Laundries." They had three locations, according to documents from the Detroit Historical Society. Another venture was a housing development project that Bob (Jack's youngest son) mentioned in *The Family Histories*. He wrote how Jack was sent to Detroit by Gideon to "oversee the development of a housing project on a race track property owned by Gideon." Paul also wrote about the race track property in a section included in his brother's histories document, saying that the race track project "went badly" after the 1929 stock market crash. I was unable to verify the housing project or Gideon's ownership of a race track.

Jack's ventures in Detroit were short-lived. A few days after the 1929 stock market crash, he and his wife Anne [Cora] and their two sons, Paul and Richard, were in a tragic car accident in London, Ontario, while en route to Wiarton from Detroit. Their second-born son, Richard [Dickie], died in the accident from a fractured skull, according to his death certificate. He was one-year old. The family never returned to Michigan, though Jack, according to Bob's family history document, went back in the early 1940s to try and locate his business partner. Jack thought the business might be worth some money. His search was unsuccessful.

Jack and his family relocated to Wiarton the year following the accident after Anne [Cora] was discharged from the hospital. Soon after, Jack got a job working for Gideon, who at the time was part owner and superintendent [general manager] of the Wiarton Furniture Factory. Jack worked as bookkeeper and sales manager, but in 1936, after a spate of management strife, both he and Gideon were let go. Jack, with the help of Gideon, got a job at the Beach Furniture Company in Cornwall as sales manager (by then, there was a third son, Bob). After a short year in Cornwall, for reasons never revealed, Jack and his family returned to Wiarton. Without many job options, Jack started Kastner Clothing Store, also known as Kastner Menswear Store, on Berford Street in Wiarton in 1939. According to family sources, the store never experienced great success.

### (Chief) Thomas L. Boyle (1903 – 1983)

Chief Boyle left Wiarton three years after Gretchen's death. He had served as Wiarton's police chief since 1940. He moved with his wife and daughter to New York State in 1945 and appeared to leave policing altogether. His occupation was listed as "salesman" in the 1950 US Census in Jefferson, NY. Boyle died in 1983 in New York State. It is unclear what prompted him to leave Wiarton. It may have been family-driven, as documents show that Boyle had a brother living in New York. Perhaps Gretchen's death was a factor in his leaving Wiarton and policing. However, this is speculative.

### Hillcrest (1885 – present)

Hillcrest, located at 394 Gould Street, housed the Kastner

family until 1959. After Gideon passed away in 1949, Annie and Margaret lived in the home until Annie's death in 1959. Hillcrest was sold that year to the Buchanan family. They made several modifications to the home (not necessarily improvements) that included removing a large room that was attached to the south wall. The room had been used as a summer kitchen during the Kastner family tenure (1912 – 1959), and as a greenhouse, and possibly a conservatory by the first owners, the Kyles, who lived at Hillcrest between 1885 and 1903.

Victor Last purchased Hillcrest from the Buchanans in 1971. At that time, the house was in a sad state of disrepair. There were several rumours within the neighbourhood about the Buchanans, including one that stated a family member had attempted to drive a motorcycle up the stairs of Hillcrest and ended up in the hospital. The rumour however, could not be verified.

It took several years for the Last family to restore the home to its former state. In recent years, Victor has replaced the wrap-around porch, added a split rail fence, built several intricate gardens, and added an assortment of garden statues—all of which enhance the home's stately exterior.

Hillcrest, Wiarton. August 2021

Beginning in the late 1970s and up until 2018, Victor operated Hillcrest as a Bed & Breakfast. My husband and I and our youngest two children stayed in Hillcrest in 2012.

Victor has since become a close friend. He encouraged me to write Gretchen's story. His research support and photographs have been central to this book. Victor's passion and enthusiasm for the Bruce Peninsula, as well as his talent as a photographer, author, historian, and archivist, have enriched countless people's lives.

Victor, at the time of this book's publication, lives at Hillcrest with his youngest son and his son's family.

### Doctor S. J. Stott (1898 – 1965)

Doctor Stott left town three months after Gretchen's death. He was one of the few practicing physicians in Wiarton in 1941. He shared a medical office with his wife, Dr. Nita Kinsella-Stott, a dentist. They opened their joint office in 1926 in Wiarton's Perkin's Building. Yet on September 4, 1941, three months after Gretchen's death, both doctors announced they were moving their practices to Toronto. It is unclear why. My guess is that Gretchen's suicide was a factor. Wiarton was a small town—Dr. Stott may have felt partially responsible, and possibly the townspeople may have felt the same way.

### Gideon Litt Kastner (1865 – 1949)

A few years after Gretchen's death, Gideon's health declined. According to Bob's family history document, Gideon was diagnosed with Parkinson's disease sometime after Gretchen's death, and according to Bob, spent "much time in bed until his death." Gideon's funeral was held at St. Paul's Presbyterian Church, with over 300 people in attendance. He was interred at Bayview Cemetery in Wiarton.

The opening lines of Gideon's obituary in *The Wiarton Echo* seem to capture how Gideon was viewed by the community, "Prominent citizen Gideon Kastner passes…his death removes a leader in the industrial, political, and social life, not only of the town of Wiarton, but of the whole County of Bruce."

Gideon started his career in lumber—he bought one of the first sawmills in Wiarton in 1894, purchased the lumber rights to various parcels of land in the surrounding area, and founded Kastner Lumber Company. His lumber empire, at its height, produced up to three million board feet of lumber per year. His business interests soon expanded beyond lumber; he partnered with David Porter a local businessman involved in construction. Together, they secured bids and built numerous breakwaters and harbours within Georgian Bay, as well as engaging in several dredging projects.

Gideon's involvement in the community was extensive. He served several terms as Wiarton's mayor, reeve, and city councillor, and was Chairman of Wiarton's Board of Education for over sixteen years. Serving as President of Wiarton's Board of Trade was another role, as were others within Wiarton's Presbyterian Church that included chairmanship of the board. Gideon was also known for his support of recreation in Wiarton—he was one of the Oliphant Campers Association's first presidents (1907-1908) and was involved in Wiarton's lawn bowling, hockey, lacrosse, and golf clubs.

It was politics however, that seemed central to Gideon's life, next to his business interests. He was an active member of the Canadian Liberal Party at all levels and was president of Wiarton's Liberal Association for several years. His political affiliations brought him close to leading figures in the Canadian Liberal Party, including Prime Minister Mackenzie King. Gideon established a close friendship with the prime minister, and according to Bob, Gideon was offered an appointment to the Canadian Senate. He declined and instead was appointed Honorary Price and Trade Commissioner for Western Ontario, a position he held for several years.

Family played an important role in Gideon's life it seems. Of the family members I met, all spoke highly of him. Bob also wrote that Gideon was his idol and that he always had time for his grandchildren. Several family photographs capture Bob's sentiment. One picture shows Gideon holding an infant grandchild affectionately. In another (below), Gideon is holding the hands of his grandson, the only son of Isobel—both are smiling.

Gideon, though, according to rumours, had a vice—gambling. Lore suggests that Gideon won Hillcrest in settlement of a gambling debt. Though the story could not be verified, it is described in the "Town of South Bruce Peninsula's Heritage Walking Tour" brochure, which features Hillcrest as one of the town's architecturally notable homes. True or not (likely not), the story does not take away the fact that Gideon was an enterprising, generous man.

Gideon and his grandson Clive. c. 1945

MABEL DUNCAN (NEE MORROW) (1893 – 1945)
Mabel was the editor of Wiarton's newspaper, *The Canadian Echo*, when Gretchen died. She had been editor since 1936—a role she had taken over after the death of her husband, Edward A. Duncan, who had been editor at the time.
The paper had gone through several name changes by 1941 and would return to its original name, *The Wiarton Echo*, in December 1941 from *The Canadian Echo*. Mabel continued as editor for four more years until her unexpected death in 1945. She was fifty-two years old. Mabel's son, Edward, Jr., took over as the newspaper's editor after her death.
Mabel was remembered in her obituary as a "power in her community." Power is a good word to describe Mabel—my research revealed that she was one of the few, if not the only female newspaper editor in Canada in the period when she worked as chief editor at Wiarton's newspaper between 1936 and 1945.

MARGARET LILLIAN MILLS (NEE KASTNER) (1897 – 1965)
Margaret lived in her family home, Hillcrest, with her mother Annie until Annie died in 1959. After the house was sold, Margaret moved to an apartment in Wiarton in an area Bob described in his family history document as the "flats." She died alone in her apartment in a fire on December 25, 1965. Her death certificate states "careless smoking" as the cause. Bob, who lived a short distance from Margaret's apartment at the time, recounted seeing smoke billowing out of Margaret's apartment windows on the evening of December 24.
Margaret's life story is intriguing but difficult to put together. One certainty is that she, like her brother Jack, had a problem with alcohol. It is also possible, according to family stories that Margaret suffered from anxiety or other emotional disturbances. One perplexing part of Margaret's life is her brief marriage to Charles Edward Mills. Mills was fifteen years her senior. They married in 1931. On the marriage certificate, Mills' occupation

is listed as "broker" and Margaret's as "domestic." According to voter lists, it appears they lived together for at least three years after their marriage in Stokes Bay, Ontario—Mills' hometown. But they separated, and Margaret returned to Hillcrest, according to family stories. This was verified by voter lists, including one from 1938 that shows Margaret back in Wiarton and her occupation as "nurse." In 1949, Margaret is listed as "widow" and in 1957 as "spinster." She and Mills never divorced. It is not clear how they met, or the cause of their separation.

GRETCHEN HELEN DOULL (NEE KASTNER) (1907 - 1941)
Gretchen was buried in Bayview Cemetery, less than a kilometre from Hillcrest. Her grave was several feet from where the rest of the Kastner family would eventually rest. Her tombstone read: "Doull; Sacred to the memory; Gretchen; Kastner-Doull; 1907 - 1941." When my family and I visited Wiarton in 2012, tree branches from a nearby tree covered much of Gretchen's headstone, and moss had invaded the grooves on the stone's lettering. While there, we cut back the branches, scrubbed the stone, and planted flowers. We also discovered that Gretchen was included on her parents' tombstone: "Kastner; In abiding memory of; Gideon Litt Kastner; 1865 - 1949; His Beloved Wife; Annie Symon Kastner 1870 - 1959; Their Beloved Daughter; Gretchen Helen 1907 - 1941; Until The Day Break."

Gretchen met my grandfather Robert while she was attending a two-year program at Macdonald College in Montreal, and Robert was studying mechanical engineering at McGill University. Macdonald College at that time (1928 - 1929) was a sister school to McGill, located 32 kilometres from its campus. Macdonald had three schools then: the School of Agriculture, the School for Teachers, and the School of Household Science. The latter offered two non-degree programs: Homemaker's and Institutional Administration. Gretchen was in the Institutional Administration program, according to McGill's 1929 yearbook. She was also a member of the Women's Macdonald College Athletic Association. Robert was on McGill's Mechanical Engineering soccer team that same year. My guess is that is how they met—through sports. They married in October 1929, the same year Robert graduated, and, presumably, Gretchen.

One of my research questions about Gretchen was whether she worked or had a career. It seemed likely, not only because of her schooling but also because there was a six-year gap between when she and Robert married and when Hugh was born. I found one clue from their marriage certificate: Gretchen's occupation is recorded as dietitian. Her career choice appears to align with her schooling, as dietetics has its roots in Home Economics, which was taught at Macdonald College. As a profession, dietetics started in Canada in 1902, with jobs mostly in hospitals. Gretchen may have worked in the field while living in Montreal, but that is lost to history. The only other documented evidence I uncovered regarding Gretchen's activities in Montreal was in Branksome Hall's 1938 yearbook, *The Slogan*. It mentioned Gretchen as one of the attendees at a luncheon with the Branksome Hall Alumni Association at the Winter Club in Montreal in November 1937.

### Robert Morse Doull (1907 - 1995)

After Gretchen's funeral, my grandfather, Robert, took Heather and Hugh back with him to Montreal. The children lived with Robert's parents for a full year in Halifax, Nova Scotia. During that year Robert was busy—he bought a large house in Westmount (a suburb of Montreal) and married Nina Youmatoff on April 11, 1942. They were married in a Russian Orthodox church in Montreal. Nina was twenty-six, and my grandfather was thirty-five. Shortly after the wedding, Hugh and Heather returned to Montreal to live with their father and new stepmother, Nina. Nina's parents, Olga and Serge, also moved in with the newly established family. Robert and Nina eventually added to the household—they had two boys a few years later.

Robert continued working as an engineer at Dominion Engineering Works in Montreal after marrying Nina, though Nina had by then discontinued her job at Dominion as a stenographer.

He also had wanted to join the armed forces in World War II, but Robert's role at Dominion Engineering was considered essential to the war effort. The company manufactured components used in war machinery, which included bearings (the division Robert worked in), hydraulic turbines, and high-pressure gear pumps, among others.

Robert, my grandfather, never spoke of Gretchen, though I wish that I had asked him about her before he passed away.

### HEATHER MARY MARGARET DOULL (1940 – 2022); HUGH DOULL (1934 – 2012)

Heather and Hugh were in contact with their Doull grandparents as children, but not with their Kastner grandparents or family. Gretchen's sister, Isobel, had wanted to adopt her niece and nephew after Gretchen's death, but her efforts were unsuccessful. She attempted to keep in touch with Hugh and Heather when they were children by sending gifts and letters for birthdays and Christmas', which Hugh and Heather did not recall receiving.

As adults, Heather and Hugh reconnected with some Kastner family members at a Kastner family reunion in Stratford, Ontario, in 2007. It was Hugh who found out about the reunion and invited my Mum. Hugh also visited Hillcrest around the same time. After the reunion, Mum established a friendship with her cousin, Martha [the eldest daughter of Isobel], who coincidentally, was living close to Mum in Toronto. During that year, Mum met her aunt Isobel. When Mum moved to Oakville from Toronto soon after, she hosted a dinner gathering at her apartment, inviting Isobel and her three children, who were all born after Gretchen died: Clive, Martha, and Sheila. I was there with my family, as were my two sisters. I don't remember much from the event, but I do remember Aunt Isobel as well-spoken and elegant. In hindsight, I wish I had asked her more questions about Gretchen—what she was like as a child, as a sister, and as a woman.

I believe Mum was haunted by her mother's death. How could she not be? Mum never spoke resentfully of Gretchen but did of her stepmom. I would get frustrated when she spoke ill of Nini, but in hindsight, it's not surprising given the complexity of their relationship. I know that my step-grandmother loved Mum as Mum did her.

My mum passed away on May 27 [2022]—the same date that Gretchen died (even though Gretchen's death certificate states May 28, I believe she died the night before). In the wake of losing my mum, I found this comforting.

ANNIE ROBERTA KASTNER (NEE SYMON) (1870 – 1959)
Annie did not play a starring role in family stories, nor was much written about her in *The Family Histories*. I did gather, however, that Annie was a kind woman, active in her church, opposed alcohol, and, according to Bob, "made a great schnitzel pie." Her obituary in Wiarton's paper stated, "The late Mrs. Kastner played a prominent part in the life of the community and was widely known for her kindness and hospitality. She was a very active and devoted member of St. Paul's Presbyterian Church. She was a life member of the Women's Missionary Society and honorary president of the Young Women's Service Club of the church."

ANNE CORA KASTNER (NEE GARDINER) (1903 – 1984)
Anne [Cora] took over operations of the menswear store upon Jack's death in 1953. In 1956, her son Bob assumed store operations until 1973, at which time the store was either sold or closed. Anne eventually moved to Copper Cliff, Ontario, for a teaching position. She returned to Wiarton a few years later for a position in the English Department at Wiarton's high school. Anne retired in Wiarton, then Niagara-on-the-Lake, and died there in 1984 at

the age of eighty-one.

Anne had been severely injured in the car accident in London, the same one in which their son, Richard [Dickie], was killed. She was in the hospital for a full year after the crash. She underwent multiple surgeries on her right leg in the years following. According to her sons, Anne was a positive and energetic force, despite the limitations caused by the accident. Gideon was said to be very kind to his daughter-in-law, which Anne's sisters-in-law, according to Bob and Paul, resented.

As a young woman, Anne was one of the few women in Wiarton who held a university degree; she graduated from one of the University of Toronto's undergrad programs and from the university's teacher's college.

### DOCTOR ROY HACKING (1875 – 1944)

Doctor Hacking continued with his medical practice in Tara, Ontario, until his death in 1944. Tara is 32 kilometres south of Wiarton. Dr. Hacking was the Medical Officer of Health for Tara and Arran Township (part of Grey-Bruce County), which would have made him a logical second choice for the role of coroner on May 28, 1941, when a Wiarton doctor was unavailable.

Though it could not be verified, it is likely that Dr. Hacking and Gideon knew each other, as suggested in the book, due to both men's prominence in the community.

# AFTERWORD

Life events and tragedies do not occur in a vacuum. Cultural factors, societal values, and current events are woven into the fabric of a life story. Following are unique factors and events that occurred during Gretchen's lifetime that are part of her story, her family's, and those who were impacted by her death.

ALCOHOL: PROHIBITION and DRINKING PASSPORTS

PROHIBITION
Alcohol in Canada has a complicated history. Canada was one of several countries engulfed by temperance movements at the beginning of the twentieth century. The movements promoted moderation in alcohol consumption or complete abstinence due to alcohol's perceived destructive effects: drunkenness and spouses who drank away their pay cheques (mostly husbands). While the United States was completely "dry" from 1920 to 1933, during a similar time frame in Canada, alcohol could be produced and distributed but not sold in most provinces. Under the British North America Act, provinces had control over their own liquor sales. This led to a strange phenomenon—in Ontario, for example, from 1919 to 1927, alcohol could not be purchased in retail outlets or sold in bars or restaurants, but its production was legal. To complicate matters, consuming alcohol was allowed in

private residences, but it could only be obtained with a doctor's prescription.

The complexities around alcohol are what make the photograph *Full of Hooch* (below) with Gretchen and her friends intriguing. First, because hooch was a term used for illicit liquor, and second, because the photo was taken sometime between 1922 and 1924—during Ontario's Prohibition. The girls would have been between fifteen and seventeen years old. I wondered: what would have motivated Gretchen and her friends to pretend to be intoxicated while holding bottles of (presumably) liquor and photograph it? A prank, maybe inspired by a desire to make fun of the Protestant-driven movement or maybe because of discussions they heard about alcohol among their parents and possibly in church. During Gretchen's teen years, most Protestants (as the Kastners were) viewed alcohol as an evil—a hindrance to a good and moral society.

Ironically, Ontario, which was predominantly Protestant, produced the most alcohol in Canada during the 1920s through the 1940s. It had six large distilleries and twenty-nine breweries. Quebec, at least during Prohibition, was one of Ontario's largest customers for alcohol. Quebec was an anomaly—their ban on liquor sales had lasted only a few months in 1919. The United States was another customer, although an illegal one.

The city of Detroit would have been a port of entry for Ontario's illegal booze, which was fortunate for Jack when he was living there in the midst of United States Prohibition. Speakeasies would have been plentiful. But for those in small towns (like Wiarton), getting hold of 'hooch' would have been more of a challenge.

In Ontario, by 1927, Prohibition was over. Alcohol was legal, but sales and distribution were taken over by a government entity—the Liquor Control Board of Ontario (LCBO). Its aim was two-fold: to regulate the sales and distribution of alcohol and to "promote temperance and home training" (LCBO Annual Report, 1927). The goal of home training was to "promote drinking in moderation and within one's financial means". For better or worse, control over alcohol in Ontario had changed hands from that of temperance advocates to the politicians.

DRINKING PASSPORTS VIA LIQUOR PERMIT BOOKS

When Jack returned from Detroit to Wiarton in 1929, he could legally purchase liquor in the government-run LCBO store or Brewers' Warehouse, but he, like all other Ontario residents, required a liquor permit to buy beer, spirits, or wine. Buying booze was now a tightly controlled privilege. Permits, issued by the LCBO, were granted after an approval process. Each permit had a unique, six-digit code tied to the permittee's identity. Similar to a passport, but instead of pages for immigration officials' stamps, they had columns for LCBO employees to record purchase details: date, alcohol type, quantity, and dollar value. Store clerks completed corresponding purchase order forms with the permittee's details, which were then tallied, compiled, and sent to the LCBO's head office for analysis each week. All permittees were subject to an investigation and the potential withdrawal of alcohol privileges if purchases were deemed excessive.

This system brings up the question—how did Jack and others like him, who might not fall in line with the government's view of moderation, skirt the system? Research revealed loopholes. For one, someone else could purchase liquor for another individual by using his or her permit. Likely, it would have been a male because women who worked in the home (as most did) were tied to their husband's credentials. According to the LCBO, the occupation of housewife "tells us nothing" (LCBO Circular no. 1159, 1930). A more likely loophole Jack used was the single-purchase permit. Customers could buy a single-use permit at the LCBO store for twenty-five cents—no strings attached. "A small quantity of liquor can be purchased... no more than twelve bottles" (LCBO Annual Report, 1934–35). Granted, twelve bottles seem like a large quantity, but my research revealed no data on bottle sizes.

There was, however, considerable criticism over the single permit's perceived laxity. The system was terminated in 1942. Jack likely found another loophole.

In 1962, nine years after Jack passed away, permit books were discontinued altogether and replaced with a less rigid system. By the early 1970s, the LCBO had dropped all requirements for customer tracking.

## DIVORCE in CANADA

Divorce in Canada up until the 1940s was rigid, discriminatory, open to public scrutiny, and difficult if not impossible to obtain. Even worse, it was overly censorious towards women, regardless of their role in the process—petitioner or respondent. In 1941, there were no federal divorce laws governing Canada, though half of the provinces had adopted their own. Ontario had done so in 1930. But dissolution of marriages was still rare. In 1938, around the time Robert was likely thinking about divorce, there were only 824 divorces granted in Ontario and 83 in Quebec. Ten years earlier, in 1928, there were 213 and 28 respectively. These numbers seem preposterous in comparison to 2019 when there were 22,377 divorces in Ontario and 9,681 in Quebec (Number of divorces, Statistics Canada, table 39-10-0051-01).

A central factor in the low divorce rates in Canada in the early twentieth century was the perception of marriage—it was considered a sanctity rooted in Christian philosophy and the church. Divorce, according to the church, was a moral failing. True for Protestants, but even more so for Catholics. Up until this time, it was the church that guided moral behaviour and societal values in Europe and, by extension, Canada. These values guided divorce laws, which led to debate and considerable angst among Canadian politicians between 1900 and 1930, when divorce was a pressing issue.

... "For my part I would rather belong to this country of Canada where divorces are few, than belong to the neighbouring republic [United States] where divorces are many. I think it argues for a good moral condition of a country where you have few divorces, even though they are made difficult—a better moral condition than prevails in a country where divorces are numerous and made easy."

— PRIME MINSTER WILFRID LAURIER speaking in a debate in the House of Commons (Canada), 1901

In Quebec, where Robert and Gretchen lived during their marriage, divorce was granted only by petition to the Parliament of Canada (as per British law). To petition for divorce, Robert or any other person seeking a divorce in Quebec or in another province without its own divorce law would have had to place a "notice of intent" in the Canadian Gazette newspaper and in two local newspapers for a period of six months. The notice had to state: the date (in Robert's case, 1929), place of the marriage (Wiarton), name and address of the petitioner (Robert; Montreal) and spouse (Gretchen), and the event surrounding the demise of the marriage (adultery). After the six-month notice period, the petition would be submitted to Parliament, where it would be reviewed, debated, and discussed among its members. If granted,

Parliament would pass an Act of Divorce nullifying the marriage.

Robert, no doubt, would not have wanted to go through the public process given his career with a prominent firm and because of his parents' notable status in Dalhousie. Fortunately for Robert, Ontario had its own judicial divorce law enacted in 1930, which offered a less public and more efficient route to divorce. Another law enacted in 1930, the Divorce Jurisdiction Act, was also in Robert's favour. It was a federal law that addressed women's legal right to seek a divorce outside the matrimonial home. Prior to this statute, a woman's domicile was considered the matrimonial home, and if a wife left, she lost all her legal rights, including the ability to petition for divorce. The Divorce Jurisdiction Act, championed by Agnes Macphail, MP for Grey-Southeast at the time, changed that. It stated:

> "A married woman... who has been living separate and apart from her husband may, in any one of those provinces of Canada in which there is a court having jurisdiction to grant a divorce, commence in the court of such province... for divorce praying that her marriage may be dissolved on any grounds that may entitle her to a divorce"
>
> — Public General Acts of Canada, 1930

Though these laws would have made it far easier for Robert to divorce Gretchen, my research turned up no records outlining his strategy. Furthermore, there was a catch with the Jurisdiction Law: the husband of the married woman must be "domiciled in the province in which such proceedings are commenced." Robert was living in Quebec, not Ontario. We will never know what his plan was, but my guess is that Gretchen moving back to Ontario was part of it, whether prompted by Robert or by Gretchen's own volition.

Sadly, but fortunately for Robert, his divorce strategy never had to be implemented because of Gretchen's death. There is no question however, that Gretchen's death would have cast a shadow over Robert and my step-grandmother's wedding when they married eleven months later.

MENTAL HEALTH in CANADA

DEPRESSION AND TREATMENT OPTIONS

Based on family stories and her suicide Gretchen was, without a doubt, suffering from severe depression. It is not clear when it began, but it was most likely triggered, or exacerbated if she were already depressed, by Robert wanting a divorce. For context, a Canadian study published in 2007 found that married individuals were four times more likely to experience a depressive episode after a marital breakdown. Given the stigma of divorce in Gretchen's era, it would have been far higher. It is also possible that Gretchen was suffering from postpartum depression—she had given birth to Heather just fourteen months prior to her death.

But the medical community was unable to help Gretchen, whatever the cause. There was little understanding of how to help depressed patients or those suffering from other emotional disorders in the early twentieth century. Women were also treated differently from men. During that time, men experiencing depression might be prescribed a holiday that included vigorous outdoor activities to recharge their bodies and minds. In contrast, women were prescribed the rest cure—bed rest, solitude, and, in some instances, high-calorie diets. Virginia Woolf, for example, was prescribed the rest cure, and as a result, her husband did not allow her to have any visitors for several weeks.

Depression, also known as melancholia and neurasthenia up until the 1940s, was frequently diagnosed in women as "hysteria." The diagnosis was applied to women who exhibited one or more symptoms that included exhaustion, nervousness, melancholia and excitably, among others. It originated with the Greeks and was introduced to modern medicine by Doctor Jean-Martin Charcot in 1880. He theorized that hysteria was exclusive to women, as per the Greeks, but was caused by an internal injury that affected their nervous system. Sigmund Freud, one of Charcot's students, took it further, suggesting that the disease was "characteristically feminine" and triggered by psychological factors, including repressed trauma.

Hysteria as a diagnosis had fallen out of favour by the 1940s, but the concept of female-specific psychological diseases did little to advance constructive treatment for patients like Gretchen who were experiencing emotional distress.

It wasn't until after World War I, when vast numbers of soldiers, mostly men, were exhibiting an array of emotional ailments, that the medical community searched in earnest for treatment options. Several were tried in the United States and Canada from the 1920s through the 1940s that included prescribing barbiturates, administering shock therapy by injecting insulin into patients, and convulsive therapy using the stimulant drug Metrazol. There was also a surgical procedure, the lobotomy, where doctors drilled through the patient's eye socket to the brain in order to cut the connection between the frontal lobe and the thalamus. This was thought to relieve patients of their ailments, but the outcomes often left patients in worsened states.

In 1938, elective convulsive therapy (ECT) was introduced—a form of shock therapy that delivered electrical currents to the patient's brain with the goal of inducing seizures. The treatment was believed to trigger a change in brain chemistry and reduce symptoms of depression and other psychiatric conditions. The procedure seems barbaric given the number of patients who experienced memory loss, cognitive confusion, and bone fractures.

The sad fact is that doctors in 1941 had few tools to address any type of emotional distress or more serious disturbances. There were numerous papers in Canadian and US medical journals in Gretchen's era describing how to treat "neurotic" disorders, which suggests that emotional ailments were of significant concern.

Fast-forward to 2024—where are we today with treating depression, addiction, anorexia nervosa, obsessive-compulsive disorder, and other emotional disturbances? We have made some progress. There are, for example, promising studies that use psychedelic substances to alleviate depression, addiction, and post-traumatic stress disorder. But there are still too few effective treatments. Prescribed drugs for psychiatric conditions have fallen far short of claims for eliminating symptoms. Side effects are numerous, and long-term efficacy is low or negligible.

More concerning is the number of treatments from Gretchen's era that are still in use today. Elective convulsive therapy is one. Another is psychosurgeries—surgeries, like lobotomies, are still considered viable treatment options. In Canada, for instance, psychosurgeries are used for treatment-resistant conditions that include OCD, severe anxiety, mood and bipolar disorders, and schizophrenia. Granted, the number of psychosurgeries performed each year is limited and according to the medical community, used as a "last resort."

On a positive note, there are more tools and resources available today than Gretchen would have had access to. There is also more dialogue around mental health at schools, workplaces, and in social settings. Yet, there is still a pressing need for comprehensive, holistic treatment options that focus on the person and not on a label or a disease.

### Anorexia Nervosa

Gretchen is described by Bob, her nephew, in *The Family Histories* as having suffered from anorexia nervosa—an eating disorder marked by restrictive eating and excessive exercise that results in low body weight. Bob wrote, "She [Gretchen] was depressed… She also suffered from anorexia." When I met Isobel, Gretchen's aunt in 2008, she also alluded to Gretchen being depressed and possibly having an eating disorder. Yet when looking at photographs of Gretchen, she appears vibrant and full of life. Except for one: a photograph (page 99) where Gretchen is wearing a bathing suit, standing on a makeshift dock by a lake with her sister Isobel in a nearby boat. Gretchen is looking up at the camera—forlorn and small.

If Gretchen were suffering from anorexia nervosa, also known as anorexia, it would have been difficult to treat. There was little understanding of the disease among families, the public, and the medical community. The disease up until the 1930s was perceived as having a biological origin given a patient's lack of appetite and low body weight. As we know today it is not a lack of appetite, but a desire to be as thin as possible combined with a fear of gaining weight.

In my research about the disorder in Gretchen's era, I discovered that two Canadian doctors, Farquharson and Hyland, had published a paper in the *Journal of American Medicine* that presented an alternate viewpoint. It was postulated that the disease was psychological in origin, not biologic, as presumed. In the paper, the doctors discussed patients who exhibited cognitive disturbances, emotional instability, obsessive behaviours, and the need for personal control, among others. They outlined a two-step treatment plan that addressed the psychological aspects of the disease.

What I found interesting was that Dr. Farquharson attended the University of Toronto Medical School at the same time as Dr. Stott—Gretchen's doctor—in 1941. Stott and Farquharson were classmates; Farquharson was one year ahead of Stott. Farquharson's paper was published in 1938, three years before Stott began treating Gretchen. I believe Stott would have read the paper, not only because it was a relevant topic published in a prominent journal but also because Farquharson was a classmate. For these reasons, I referenced Farquharson's paper in the book.

SUICIDE

Suicide is a devastating tragedy that affects family members for generations. Gretchen's family was, and is, no different. Statistics Canada published data on suicide rates beginning in 1950. In that year [1950], which was likely similar to the death rate in 1941, there were four deaths for every 100,000 of the female population. In males, it was fourteen per 100,000. The numbers have increased since then: in 2019, there were six female deaths for every 100,000, and for males, seventeen. The numbers translate to approximately twelve suicides per day in Canada.

As seen with Gretchen's story, there are people behind these numbers—men, women and sometimes children—who experienced emotional pain and distress and felt there was no way out. The impact is devastating for the victims and their families. Fortunately, today, more so than in Gretchen's time, there are resources available for individuals experiencing suicidal thoughts that include toll-free numbers for phone calls and text messaging. There are also several innovative prevention programs that have been developed by organizations that include the Zero Suicide Institute, Living Works, and the QPR Institute.

Suicide is complex, but increasing awareness and bringing topics like depression and other conditions into the open are needed for understanding, compassion, and ultimately prevention.

## WIARTON

### A Brief History

There is a truth about small towns: young people who are born in such places dream of leaving when they grow up. Wiarton was no different. Gretchen's friends—those in the photograph *Flowers of Heaven* and others—all fled town one after the other. The first to move on was Eleanor Crawford; she moved first to Berkeley, California, after high school and ended up in Montreal. Gretchen soon followed. She went to Macdonald College in Montreal where she met Robert.

Montreal was the hot spot in Canada from the 1920s through to the 1940s. It was the cultural and financial hub—a thriving metropolis with cafés, jazz venues, galleries, and clubs. It was a stark contrast to Wiarton, which was no doubt viewed by the younger generation as staid, provincial, and small.

In 1941, the population of Wiarton was 1,749, which is what Gretchen returned to with two young children, no husband, and no place to live but with her parents. In the forties, divorcees were rare, viewed with suspicion, and often denied housing, jobs, and friendship—Wiarton would have been no different.

But Wiarton was no slouch. It had a thriving port on Colpoy's Bay, with proximity to Georgian Bay and Lake Huron, well-suited for transporting the town's resources of fish and timber. It was the timber industry that had fueled Wiarton's growth beginning in the 1880s (Gideon owned one of Wiarton's first sawmills). Numerous others followed, which included: wool, roof shingles, chairs, furniture, flour, sugar (with a very costly and short-lived beet sugar factory), cement, caskets, and furniture (again). Wiarton might be described in today's language as cutting-edge—the town was continually reinventing itself economically. But in 1941, most industries, except fishing, had come and gone. The town was viewed, by Gretchen and her peers at least, as "small" in every way.

Today (2024), Wiarton's population hovers around 2,300. Its

main industries are tourism and stone mining. The two features that make Wiarton distinctive—natural stone and location—drive both. Stone quarries are more recent, but tourism was prevalent in Gretchen's era and earlier due to Wiarton's location on the Bruce Peninsula, which features stone bluffs, hiking trails, sandy beaches, and crystal-clear waters.

In June 1923, Wiarton adopted the slogan "Gateway to the Bruce Peninsula" to attract tourism due to the expansion of travel by automobile. A fitting slogan that invited visitors to discover its natural treasures. Wiarton still promotes itself as a gateway but also as the "Home of Wiarton Willie." Willie is a famous groundhog who "lives" in Wiarton and predicts, every year on February 2, the timing of spring based on the sighting (or not) of his shadow.

Wiarton Harbour with Dominion Fish Company pictured, along with lumber from local saw mills. 1912.

## Prime Minister King Visits Wiarton, 1924

Bob Kastner wrote in *The Family Histories* how Prime Minister William Mackenzie King visited Gideon and family at the Oliphant cottage during King's "first year of office" [1921 – 1922]. The visit is corroborated by Bob's brother Paul, who also described a social dance event hosted by the Oliphant Campers Association where King, from what Paul remembered, danced with his aunt Isobel. The visit aligns with King's diary, except for the date. In King's diary, the date is 1924 (Bob was off by a couple of years).

> "We left Peterborough about 3 in the morning, and were well on our way to Wiarton before I got up for breakfast... At Wiarton there was a great crowd at the station with bands, then a procession through the town which was gaily decorated with flags, bunting, etc. At the park some 2,500 were assembled, they sat in the hot sun all afternoon... After dinner [we] drove out to the shore of Lake Huron to a country dance, which was most enjoyable... At Lake Huron we saw where the water has retreated owing to the Chicago Drainage Canal."
>
> — LIBRARY AND ARCHIVES CANADA, Friday, August 29, 1924, Journal King; Handwritten — p. 243

King's diary entry didn't mention Oliphant by name, but history knows it was Oliphant given his mention of the "shore of Lake Huron." While there, King visited the Kastner family cottage, given his and Gideon's friendship, which stemmed from Gideon's leadership roles within the Liberal Party and his business interests.

King's visit to Wiarton in 1924 is indicative of Wiarton's significance in Ontario in the early decades of the twentieth century. At the time, Wiarton was a thriving industrial centre and with King's focus on manufacturing and industry as a vehicle for nation-building, the visit aligned with his political and personal interests. King's background and experience were in labour and industrial relations, dating back to his studies in university and when he served as minister of labor under Prime Minister Wilfrid Laurier.

King served six non-consecutive terms as prime minister, almost twenty-two years. To date, King is Canada's longest-serving prime minister. His last term spanned 1934–1948.

## WORLD WAR II AND WIARTON

When Gretchen returned to Wiarton in 1941, Canada was already at war with Germany, as was Britain. Prime Minister King had declared war on Germany on September 10, 1939.

The war affected every part of society in Canadian cities like Wiarton, and its effects were chronicled in Wiarton's local newspaper, *The Canadian Echo*. Throughout the war, *The Echo* described events and battles overseas, community events supporting war efforts, and news from regiments of service members from Wiarton's community.

A positive effect of the war was the economic boost it gave to Canada's economy; however, it did little to benefit Jack and his store. Many of Wiarton's men, already serving in the war, had little need for menswear. And for those who did, suits were scarce. Jack had a hard time getting inventory—clothing factories in Canada and Britain were dedicated to making army uniforms and supplies, and clothes rationing began in Britain in June 1941, further constricting supply. In his family history document, Bob wrote of a wartime memory around the store's first Christmas: "There was little promotion for the holidays as stock was limited. Handkerchiefs were the big item for Christmas gifts... The best were hung at the front... They also served as decorations."

Twenty men from Wiarton lost their lives in World War II. The names of these servicemen were added to Wiarton's War Memorial erected in 1922. The statue is featured in the background of the photograph, *Flowers of Heaven*, on page 69.

## WOMEN as PERSONS

Before and during Gretchen's lifetime, Canadian women struggled for recognition and agency in everyday situations. A stark example: women were not considered "persons" by Canadian law until 1929. The language in the British Constitution, which governed Canada until 1982, read that "he" and "they" could run for office and/or serve as elected officials. This was interpreted as excluding women and was reinforced by an 1876 ruling in Britain that stated, "Women are persons in matters of pains and penalties, but are not persons in matters of rights and privileges." This statement was challenged in 1927 by a woman seeking appointment to the Canadian Senate in a lawsuit known as the PERSONS CASE (Edwards v. A.G. of Canada). The ruling was sustained and then overturned in 1929 after a successful appeal. In 1930, Prime Minister Mackenzie King appointed the first woman to the Senate—Cairine Wilson.

The PERSONS CASE is an example of the challenges Canadian women faced in the workplace and in society. Women struggled for a voice; men ruled. Another example: Gretchen and all women in Quebec could not vote in federal elections until 1940.

There were several women who fought for women's rights during Gretchen's lifetime, including a group instrumental in the PERSONS CASE: Nellie McClung, Louise McKinney, Emily Murphy, Irene Parlby, and Henrietta Muir Edward. Another was Agnes Macphail. Macphail, born in Dundalk, Ontario, was the first woman elected to Canada's House of Commons. She worked relentlessly throughout her thirty-year political career to end legal discrimination against women in the workplace, at home, in prison, and in divorce. She was instrumental in getting Ontario's Divorce Jurisdiction Act passed into law when she was Member of Parliament for Grey-Southeast County (1921–1935), which Wiarton was part of at the time.

"I want for myself what I want for other women — absolute equality."

— Agnes Macphail

Gretchen Kastner Doull [right] at Sainte-Anne-de-Bellevue, Quebec, when she was married to Robert Doull. c. 1930–1934

# ACKNOWLEDGMENTS

This book would not have come about had it not been for my husband, Bruce, who arranged for a weekend visit in 2012 to Hillcrest, the bed and breakfast in Wiarton. Hillcrest, as described in this book, had been my grandmother's family home. Bruce's passion for his own family history extended to mine, and I'm grateful for his enthusiasm, encouragement, and research support during this project.

That weekend was a catalyst for this book, not only because of visiting Gretchen's home but also because of Hillcrest's owner, Victor Last. His passion and enthusiasm for the history of Wiarton, for the Bruce Peninsula, and for people are what moved me forward. Victor generously shared photographs, documents, his time, and energy, as well as his wide network of people who share his passion for Wiarton's history. Most importantly, Victor arranged for meetings between us and Kastner family members that included Paul Kastner (Gretchen's nephew), Sheila (Gretchen's niece), and Karen (the daughter of Gretchen's nephew—Bob).

I am grateful to Paul Kastner for sharing his memories of Gretchen with me. He was the last living family member who remembered Gretchen. Also, thanks go to Karen, who shared not only memories of her dad (Bob) but also his document, *Starting a New Life in Canada: The Family Histories,* an unpublished book devoted to the family history of the Kastners and Gardiners (Bob's mother's family). I am also grateful for Sheila, who generously shared photographs and insights into our family.

I'm also indebted to Chris Graham, founder and author of the website Postcards From the Bay, a site dedicated to the history of Wiarton and Colpoy's Bay. Chris's knowledge of Wiarton's industries and families and his willingness to share his knowledge with me and others via his website are deeply appreciated.

Victor also introduced me to the Bruce County Museum and Cultural Centre in Southampton, which holds a vast collection of historical documents and digital copies of Bruce County's families, businesses, and geographic and social history.

Another invaluable source was the book *Into the Blue: Family Secrets and the Search for a Great Lakes Shipwreck* by Andrea Curtis. The story is about a tragic shipwreck that occurred in Georgian Bay and about Curtis' grandmother, Eleanor Crawford, who was a friend of Gretchen's. Eleanor appears in several of the photographs in this book, including *Flowers of Heaven*.

# IMAGE DETAILS AND CREDITS

The majority of the book's photographs are courtesy of Victor Last of Wiarton and Sheila MacMahon, Gretchen's niece. Victor received most of the photographs of the Kastner family from Paul Kastner. I am grateful to Victor and Sheila for their generosity in sharing.

Pages 4 & 5: Long Dock, Colpoy's Bay, Don McCallum
Page 14: Isobel and Gretchen at Lake Huron, Sheila MacMahon
Page 19: Map, Colpoy's Bay, modified image from open source document
Pages 20 & 21: Gretchen's Family 1941, author; background image from *The Georgian Bay: An Account of Its Position, Inhabitants, Mineral Interests* (1893), by James Cleland Hamilton
Pages 22 & 23: The Kastner Family, Victor Last
Page 27: Paul with Heather and brother Bob on Hillcrest lawn, Victor Last
Pages 34 & 35: Jack Kastner driving motorboat, Victor Last
Page 46: Hillcrest in the 1880s, Victor Last
Page 54: Gideon Kastner, Victor Last
Page 64: Kastner siblings: (from left) Margaret, Jack, Gretchen (front), Bernice, Isobel, Victor Last

IMAGE DETAILS AND CREDITS 111

Page 69: *Flowers of Heaven*, Victor Last
Page 70: *Freaks of Humanity*, Victor Last
Page 71: Gretchen and Friends at Harbour, Victor Last
Page 72: Gretchen on Rock, Sheila MacMahon
Page 75: Gretchen and Margaret Baines, Sheila MacMahon
Page 79: Hillcrest today, Victor Last
Page 82 Gideon Kastner with grandson, Sheila MacMahon
Page 90: *Full of Hooch*, Victor Last
Page 99: Gretchen on boards with sister Isobel in boat, Sheila MacMahon
Page 101: Wiarton Harbour, Victor Last
Page 107: Gretchen at Sainte-Anne-de-Bellevue, Quebec, Sheila MacMahon

# BIBLIOGRAPHY

Beck, Earl Clifton. *Songs of the Michigan Lumberjacks*. University of Michigan Press, 1941.

Curtis, Andrea. *Into the Blue Family Secrets and the Search for a Great Lakes Shipwreck*. Random House, 2007.

Farquharson, Ray F., and Herbert H. Hyland. "Anorexia nervosa: A metabolic disorder of psychologic origin." *Journal of the American Medical Association* 111.12 (1938): 1085-1092.

Gatis, Sheila. *Wiarton, 1880-1980*. The Wiarton Echo Pub., 1980.

Genosko, Gary, and Scott Thompson. *Punched Drunk: Alcohol, Surveillance, and the LCBO 1927-1975*. Fernwood, 2010.

Gilbert, Raymond. *When Time Was a Little Slower*, Gilbert, 2003.

Goldbloom, David S. "The Early Canadian History of Anorexia Nervosa." *The Canadian Journal of Psychiatry*, vol. 42, no. 2, 1997, pp. 163–167.

Grob, Gerald N. *Mental Illness and American Society, 1875-1940*. Princeton University Press, 2019.

Kastner, Robert J. *Starting a new life in Canada: The family histories*, Kastner, (n.d.).

MacKay, Donald. *The Lumberjacks*. Natural Heritage Books, 2007.

Postcards from the Bay - History of Wiarton and Colpoy's Bay, Ontario, Chris Graham, http://postcard.wiarton.ca/intro.html.

Public General Acts of Canada, Canadian Parliament, 1930. https://archive.org/details/actsofparl1930v01cana/page/n11/mode/2up?view=theater.

Rotermann, Michelle. "Marital breakdown and subsequent depression." Statistics Canada: Health reports vol. 18,2 (2007): 33-44.

Scull, Andrew. *Desperate Remedies: Psychiatry's Turbulent Quest to Cure Mental Illness.* The Belknap Press of Harvard University Press, 2022.

Snell, James G. *In the Shadow of the Law: Divorce in Canada, 1900-1939.* University of Toronto Press, 1991.

*The Canadian Echo* [Wiarton], 29 May 1941.

*The Canadian Echo* [Wiarton], 5 June 1941.

Thompson, John Herd, and Allen Seager. *Canada, 1922-1939: Decades of Discord.* McClelland and Stewart, 1990.

Tone, Andrea. "Listening to the Past: History, Psychiatry, and Anxiety." *The Canadian Journal of Psychiatry*, vol. 50, no. 7, 2005, pp. 373–380.

Printed in the USA
CPSIA information can be obtained
at www.ICGtesting.com
LVHW052107120424
777208LV00020B/531